Exotic Shorthair Cats

Marianne Mays

contents

Acknowledgments

Many thanks must go to the following:

Christine Wilson (Pometta Cats) for help, advice and the use of her excellent booklet *The Exotic Shorthair – its development in the UK.*

Christina Carpenter (Milagro Exotics) for letting us use of some of her beautiful Exotics as photographic models, and also for help and advice.

Alan Robinson, LMPE, for his brilliant photographs.

The Governing Council of the Cat Fancy (GCCF) for the use of their breed standards.

To all the breeders, exhibitors and owners of Exotics who supplied me with photographs or allowed my husband, Nick, to photograph their cats.

Dale Briggs, owner of the Paws for Thought Cat Emporium in Leeds, Yorkshire, for allowing his range of feline products to be photographed.

Chris Robinson, MRCVS, for being such a patient model.

All photographs not otherwise acknowledged were taken by Nick.

I would like to dedicate this book to the memory of Blondie (Adkrilo Tasmine) 1988–1997, who was not an Exotic at all, but who was my first pedigree cat and the start of it all.

Littermates – Shaded Silver female Blondbella Moonshine Magic (left) and Silver Tabby Variant male Blondbella Spice of Life (right).

introducing the 1
exotic shorthair

Patrystar Munchkin, an early Exotic, born in 1988. His type is very different from that seen today. Owned and bred by Pat Brice. Photograph by Sheila Harrison.

What is an Exotic?

'What sort of cat is that?' people ask, pointing to one of my Exotics. 'It's an Exotic,' I reply. 'Yes, I can see that it's very exotic, but what breed is it?' is the invariable response.

The Exotic, or Exotic Shorthair, is the official breed name for a cat which is not very well known outside cat circles, but which is rapidly gaining in popularity. Some people believe that one day it may be even more popular than the Persian and the British Shorthair.

page 5: Milagro Bambino, owned by Christina Carpenter. Photograph by Alan Robinson

Patrystar Bugsey (right), a rare Cream and White Harlequin Pattern Exotic, next to a British Shorthair. Owned and bred by Pat Brice. Photograph by P. Brice.

What exactly is an Exotic? Probably the best description is that the Exotic is a shorthaired Persian, in other words, a cat of the same type and build as the Persian, but without the long fur. The body is short and heavy, the legs sturdy, the tail short, and the head is broad with small, rounded ears and a flat face. The fur differs from most other shorthaired cats in that it is very dense, slightly longer than the fur seen on most cats, and does not lie completely flat, but stands out from the body. The cat's temperament is very similar to that of the Persian; it is friendly and laid back – a loving, purring lap cat. But the Exotic has a more active, playful nature than that commonly associated with Persians. The Exotic is a breed with many nicknames, such as 'The Teddybear cat', 'The Persian in a mini-skirt', 'The Persian without pain', or 'The lazy man's Persian'. The latter two refer to the fact that this is a breed ideal for those who admire the look and personality of the Persian cat, but who feel that they could not cope with the enormous amount of grooming that the Persian demands.

Champion Adouzsh Jackolacotte, one of the breed's first Champions.

UK Gr Ch Owletts Maverick, a Red Tabby male, was the first Exotic GCCF champion in the breed.

The History of the Exotic

The Exotic was developed independently, first in the United States and later in Great Britain. The common factor in both cases was that the breed was developed purely by chance, using cats that were considered to be useless side products in the breeding of other cats.

Breeders of American Shorthair cats wanted to improve the type of their cats, and decided to use Persians as outcrosses in their breeding programmes. Some of the kittens born as a result of this cross-mating had a type which was too Persian (a flat face, for example) to suit the American Shorthair, and also a coat that was not quite right for this breed. Although deemed unsuitable for further American Shorthair breeding, some breeders liked the kittens for what they were and continued to breed from them. Eventually a Persian-type cat with short, dense fur was developed: the Exotic. The breed gained recognition in 1966, with full championship status in 1967.

In Britain, the Exotic was developed in a very similar manner. Breeders of British Shorthairs used Persians as outcrosses to improve the type of their cats. Some of the resulting kittens were rejected as they were found to have a too-flat face and a too-soft coat to be of any use in the British Shorthair programme. As in the United States, some breeders liked these new-look cats and bred from them. Rather than use British Shorthairs, they mated the shorthaired kittens to Persians to maintain the Persian type. The Exotic Shorthair was thus developed.

The first club for this new breed, the Exotic Cat Club, was formed in 1983 and a second, the Exotic Shorthair Breeders' Society, the following year. Both clubs are still going strong today. However, it took quite a number of years before the breed gained full recognition and championship status with the country's largest registering body, the Governing Council of the Cat Fancy (GCCF).

Before 1986, breeders and owners of Exotics were able to exhibit their cats at shows only to let the public see the cats, without being able to compete in the show. In 1986, the Exotic gained Preliminary status from the GCCF, which meant that the cats could be shown in competition at cat shows all over the country. To gain Preliminary status, the Exotic breeders had to make an application to the GCCF which contained: a suggested preliminary standard of points for the breed; a breeding policy outlining which breeds had been used to create the new breed; details of how the new breed differed from established breeds; what purpose this new breed could serve.

When the Exotic gained Preliminary status, it was shown in special Assessment classes. In these classes the cats are not placed first, second, third, and so on, but are judged to the breed's Standard of Points, a copy of which each exhibitor has to supply with their cat. Only if the judge considered the cat to be a good example of its breed would it be awarded a Merit certificate. The Exotics

As youngsters, Blue Exotics sometimes show uneven colouring.
Photograph by Alan Robinson.

The Exotic's eyes are a striking feature of the breed. Photograph by Alan Robinson.

were now able to enter various side classes (see chapter 5) where they competed against Persians and were awarded graded placings as in normal competition.

It was then up to the breeders to show their cats to gain Merit Certificates and achieve Provisional status, the next step up the ladder towards full recognition of the breed. Before Provisional status is granted, at least 30% of all registered cats within the breed have to gain at least four Merit certificates each. These Merit certificates must be awarded by four different judges, and only two won as a kitten count. (All four, however, can be gained as adults.) The Exotic finally reached this stage in 1992, when the breed was granted Provisional status. By

Bonvisage Millymollymandy, a Dilute Tortie/White Exotic Shorthair.
Owned by Margaret Boniface.

Gr Pr Patrystar Cherryblossom, one of the Exotics who won three ICs to enable the granting of Championship status. Bred by Pat Brice, owned by Linda and Roy Dowley. Photograph by P. Brice.

now over 100 breeders were working on the Exotic. Over 450 Merit certificates were awarded to Exotics during the six years of Preliminary status. The first Exotic to win a Merit was the Self Blue male, Soulsease Starborn, owned and bred by Elissa Coleman Smith. The first female Merit winner was Soulsease Sin Tillate, a Blue-Cream also bred by Mrs Coleman Smith, owned by Marion Dimmock. This cat also became one of the first two Blue-Creams to win three Merits.

Once the Exotic gained Provisional status, it got its own open classes at Championship cat shows, where the cats competed against each other and were awarded first, second and third placings. There is a breed class each for males and females as adults, kittens and neuters respectively. The winner of each adult and neuter breed class could gain an Intermediate Certificate (IC) if deemed good enough by the judge. Twenty percent of all registered Exotics needed to gain at least three ICs each, awarded under three different judges, for the breed to gain full recognition – Championship status. The very first Exotics to be awarded ICs were Donceur Cheeky Charlie, a Black male owned and bred by Mrs G Obringer, and the female Pometta Strawbry Shortcake, a Blue-Cream bred by Mr and Mrs Wilson, latterly owned by Gloria Dent. The first neuter winning an IC was Mr T Jones Bartos' York Oliver Lawson, a Red Tabby.

Towards the end of 1994, the final criteria were fulfilled and the GCCF granted the breed Championship status, taking effect from 1 June 1995. Now the Exotic was fully recognised and of equal standing with any other breed. The most exciting part of this was that, finally, Exotic cats had the opportunity to gain titles such as Champion and Premier. The first Challenge Certificate (CC) winners, who gained their awards just a few days after the breed was fully recognised, were Owletts Maverick, a Red Tabby male owned by Mr and Mrs Clarke, bred by Mrs Rosemary Fisher, and Krissan Betty Boop, a female Tortiepoint Colourpoint, owned and bred by Mrs Chris Simpson. The first neuter to gain a Premier Certificate (PC) was Robwen Cream Cracker, a Cream male owned and bred by Mrs Eirwyn Roberts. Maverick later went on to become Champion Owletts Maverick, the breed's very first champion. The breed's first Premier was Pr. Icemoor Barney Rubble, a Cream female owned and bred by Mrs Shelagh Heavens. The first Grand CC was eventually awarded to Maverick, who also became the first UK Grand Champion.

The first breed show solely for Exotics in Great Britain was staged by the Exotic Cat Club at Lutterworth, Leicester in September 1994. The show attracted an entry of around 50 cats, and Best in Show was awarded to Victorious Springsteen, a glamorous Orange Eyed White male owned by Mr and Mrs Walker, bred by Gloria Dent. Springsteen is the son of the first female IC winner, Pometta Strawbry Shortcake, and the grandson of the very first Merit winner, Soulsease Starborn.

The eyes of a five-week-old kitten have not yet changed colour.

buying
your exotic 2

Cats in general, and Exotics in particular, make excellent pets for young and old alike. However, there are always people for whom cats are not suitable. Before buying your cat, ask yourself the following questions. First, and most importantly, you should consider whether you are prepared to care for a cat during all of its natural life. A cat normally lives for around 12 or 13 years, but some may live up to 20 years. Cats do not demand as much care and attention as many other pets because they are fairly independent animals, but they still need feeding, grooming, and so on.

The next question is that of cost. An Exotic is quite expensive to buy, and then you have to add the cost of the equipment it needs. There are the running costs of feeding, and veterinary bills. At the very least, you need to pay for annual vaccinations, and for neutering if you do not intend to breed from your cat. If your cat falls ill, further veterinary treatment will be necessary which can be costly. Do consider taking out pet insurance, as this greatly helps to reduce veterinary costs. Your local veterinary surgery can provide you with details of the various insurance companies that specialise in pet insurance.

Patrystar Crystal Tips is a dilute Tortie/White Van Variant.
Variants are born in most litters.
Owned by Margaret Boniface. Photograph by M. Boniface.

Page 17: Four-month-old Pometta SomethingSpecial, a Silver Spotted Exotic.
Owned and bred by John and Christine Wilson. Photograph by C Wilson.

The Exotic can be as quiet and relaxed as a Persian...
Breeder and photographer: Christina Carpenter.

Will everyone in your family welcome a cat? It is important that everybody agrees with the purchase so that the cat is wanted by all. Once I was visited by a woman wanting to view a litter of kittens, who stated that she personally couldn't stand cats but her children wanted one so she had given in to their pleas. This is not an ideal situation in which to bring up a cat. A pet must feel wanted in order to be happy and well behaved. Are you or anyone close to you allergic to cats? You do not want to bring a new kitten home, only to find that you cannot keep it due to allergy.

What about other pets? Most dogs can be taught to tolerate cats, and many make very good friends with them. However, there are dogs that will never accept a cat in the same house. Make sure that your dog isn't a cat hater before bringing a kitten home. Other cats need not present a problem, as most adult cats accept a new kitten in due course. Small pets such as hamsters and gerbils must be kept in secure cages out of the cat's reach, preferably in a locked room, as all cats are natural hunters that cannot be taught not to kill small animals. The same goes for birds: either you keep the birds in a separate room which the cat cannot get into, or you make sure they are out of the cat's reach. Bigger pets, such as rabbits and guinea pigs, are usually no problem as they are slightly too big for the average cat to chase and kill.

The Exotic as a Pet

Never choose a cat simply because of its looks, as temperament and behaviour vary between the different breeds. Being a hybrid, the Exotic possesses the behaviour pattern of both its Persian and shorthair ancestors. One moment your Exotic may behave just like a Persian; a quiet, loving cat content to stay asleep on your lap for most of the evening, with a few moments of gentle play in between. The next it may decide to become more of an extrovert, charging around the house chasing a ball or a fly. The Exotic really has the best of both worlds.

The Exotic is not a very vocal cat. You get the occasional 'miaow', but will be spared the running commentary that is common in the oriental breeds such as the Siamese.

The Exotic as Show Cat

As a show cat, the Exotic has many advantages over its Persian cousins. It does not need extensive grooming, so its preparation is much easier. After a moult the Exotic may well be 'out of coat', which means that the coat is less dense than usual and lies flat against the body, which is a fault. However, it does not take as long for an Exotic to regain its coat as it does for a Persian. The Exotic can be put on the show bench for a longer period of time each year than a longhaired cat, but there may be a few weeks or months when it will not look its best, unlike most shorthaired breeds. Having a very placid, easy-going temperament, the Exotic does not usually mind being shown, and settles down quite happily for a snooze in its show pen. Generally, judges find the Exotic easy to handle.

Buying an Exotic

Once you have decided that an Exotic is the cat for you, where do you look for your kitten? Read books about cat care, talk to breeders and visit cat shows. Although the Exotic is becoming more popular, it is still comparatively rare. You will not be able to find an Exotic kitten easily, so be prepared to wait for the kitten you want. Most kittens are born in the spring, so more are available in the early summer than later in the year.

... or be ready to play, like Bonvisage Mighty Mouse, owned and photographed by Margaret Boniface...

You are not likely to find Exotics in pet shops and, even if by chance you do, it is better to buy a kitten from the person who actually bred it, so that you can see the kitten with its mother and find out how it was reared. To get in touch with reputable breeders, read the advertisements in any of the cat magazines, such as *Cats* and *Cat World*. You can also contact one of the Exotic breed clubs. Most breed clubs run kitten lists but, if no kittens are available currently, the clubs can give you details of breeders to contact so that you can put your name down on their waiting lists. You can reach the breed clubs by contacting the relevant governing body of the cat clubs in the country where you live (see Useful Addresses on page 140).

Tell the breeder why you want a kitten. Do you want a pet, or do you wish to show and eventually breed from it? Kittens are normally classified in one of three categories: pet quality, breeding quality and show quality. A pet-quality kitten is just that, a friendly, healthy kitten that makes a lovely pet but is not quite up to show or breeding standards. A breeding-quality kitten is one that is not quite good enough to put on the show bench, but whatever fault it possesses is so slight that the breeder assumes it will not be passed on in breeding. For example, a lovely coloured cat with the correct coat quality but a too-long face may produce beautiful show-quality kittens when bred to a cat with a shorter face. Finally, a show-quality kitten is one that closely resembles the written breed standards; a kitten that the breeder feels could do well on the show bench. This kitten is, of course, also suitable to breed from, and makes a good pet as well. There is nothing that says you have to exhibit a show-quality kitten, although most breeders like

... or be ready to explore. Dolina NoFrills Floella is ready for anything. Owned, bred and photographed by Mrs E Dolan.

their most promising kittens to go to homes where they will have this opportunity. Bear in mind that the breeder can only give an opinion as to whether the kitten is show quality. This is by no means a guarantee that the kitten will do well on the show bench, as the breeder has no way of knowing how it will look once it has matured.

You have to pay considerably more for a show-quality kitten than a pet kitten, often twice as much. A breeding-quality kitten is often priced somewhere between the two. Exotics are still fairly expensive, so expect to pay a few hundred pounds, but remember that you are paying for a kitten that has been properly bred, fully vaccinated and is registered.

Variants

Finally, a word on Variants. All Exotics carry the Longhair gene, so some Longhaired kittens will be born in most litters. Within the GCCF, these are classified as Exotic Variants. This means that the kitten is a purebred Exotic, but that it has long fur instead of short. A Variant cannot be shown and, although you are allowed to breed from such cats, most breeders prefer not to. Therefore, the Variant kittens are sold as pets. An Exotic Variant looks just like a Persian and within some registering bodies is actually referred to as a

A pair of kittens will play together all the time.
Photograph by Margaret Boniface.

Persian. Therefore, if you decide on an Exotic because you want a shorthaired cat, do not buy a Variant. However, Variants make just as lovely pets as the 'proper' Exotics.

Male or Female?

What sex should your new kitten be? Again, this depends largely on what you want your kitten for. If all you want is a nice pet, then either sex is equally suitable as both males and females are friendly. All cats not intended for breeding should be neutered. If you want to show your cat but not breed from it, then again either sex will do – and still have your cat neutered. There are special classes at cat shows for neutered cats, so you need not miss out on showing. If you want to breed then your choice should be a female (queen). Owning a male stud cat involves considerably more work and expense and should be not undertaken by the novice. Many cat clubs recommend that you should have been breeding regularly for at least five years before you get a stud. If you are just starting to breed, then a female should definitely be your choice. There are plenty of other breeders whose stud cats you can use for your queen.

One or Two Kittens?

Cats love company, and especially the company of other cats. Always buy two kittens if you can, as then they never feel lonely, even if you go out to work. Two kittens have endless fun together and stay playful for most of their lives whereas, when adult, a single cat stops playing and spends most of its time asleep. Two kittens are no less affectionate towards their owner than a single one.

Exotics get on well with other breeds.

Colour

Colour is a case of personal preference. Temperament does vary slightly between different coloured cats, but Exotics generally are such friendly, outgoing animals that this makes hardly any difference. Choose the colour that takes your fancy. There are many to choose from, even though some are not as readily available as others. See chapter 7 for a full description of the recognised colours in the Exotic.

Choosing Your Kitten

Pedigree cats mature slowly, and suckle their mothers for at least 10 weeks, so the kitten you choose should be no less than 12 weeks old. By then it will also have received all its initial vaccinations. Make sure that the breeder gives you all the relevant paperwork, such as vaccination certificate, pedigree, registration certificate, and preferably a diet sheet as well. If you buy your kitten simply as a pet, it may not be registered, but do check this with the breeder. If you intend to breed from your kitten, you need to make sure that it is on the correct register. The Active register is for all cats intended for breeding. A cat on the Non-active register has the words 'no progeny to be registered'

Exotics are tolerant and good-natured cats. Katy gets a hug from owner Rebecca.

written on its certificate, and no kittens from this cat are eligible for registration, other than on application (and payment of a fee) from their breeder. Cats on the Non-active register can, however, take part in cat shows.

Look carefully at the kitten you intend to buy. Does it appear friendly? Some kittens can be nervous of strangers, but this usually passes as they get used to their new home. The best way to get an indication of how your kitten will behave when adult is to look at the mother. If she is unafraid and happy to be handled, then the likelihood is that your kitten will be the same. If the mother is nervous, the kitten may well stay nervous too, so it is best to reject it.

Check for signs of good health. Does the kitten have a plump body and feel heavy? Do not pick a kitten that seems thin, or one that has a rounded stomach but a sharp edge to the back, as this could indicate worms. Is the fur clean? Check for signs of fleas or scabs, and look underneath the tail to see if the bottom is clean. Never pick a kitten which has scabs on its body, even if the breeder insists that they are only the result of play fighting; they could indicate ringworm, a fungal disease which can be transmitted to humans and other animals. Are the ears clean? A grey, waxy substance is normal, especially in longhaired cats, but the ear itself should not be red or sore and the substance should not be dark or crusty. Are the eyes bright? Exotics are flat-faced cats, and often have runny eyes because of the shape of their faces. This is quite normal; the residue can simply be wiped away, as long as the eye itself does not appear sore or red.

If you want to show your kitten, you need to satisfy yourself that it resembles the breed standard as closely as possible. You may have to take the breeder's word on this but do read up on the breed standard and study photographs. Another good way of acquainting yourself with what a good show-quality Exotic looks like is to visit some cat shows.

The Exotic and Other Cats

I mentioned earlier that you should buy two kittens rather than one, but should both these be Exotics or can you get different breeds? Usually, two cats of different breeds get on very well if both were bought as kittens. However, if you have more than two cats, and one of them is of a breed completely different to the others, then you may have a problem. It sounds unlikely, but cats can be rather 'breedist' in their attitudes! Two cats of the same breed always stick together – they seem to know without doubt which is of a particular breed, and which is not. If you have two Exotics and one Siamese, for instance, then you may find that the Siamese is bullied. Always try to mix your cats with care, so that such situations do not arise. As a hybrid, the Exotic gets on equally well with other Exotics (including Variants), Persians and British or American Shorthairs.

Bringing Your New Kitten Home

When the day finally comes to collect your Exotic, the first thing that you need is a suitable carrier. No matter how short a journey, the kitten is not safe unless transported in a proper carrier. Cat carriers come in many different versions and sizes. Choose one that is strong and secure and line it with an old towel or blanket so that the kitten has a comfortable ride.

Make sure that you choose a clean and healthy kitten. Photo by C Carpenter.

Milagro Bambino at 24 days. Photograph by Christina Carpenter.

Sit with the carrier on your lap if at all possible, and talk gently to the kitten. Most pedigree kittens should be used to journeys as they should have travelled to the vet at least twice, and so the experience will not be a new one.

At home, put the carrier on the floor in a quiet spot, open it and let the kitten venture out in its own time. Make sure that there is food, water and a litter tray nearby. It may be best to let the kitten stay in one room only during the first few days until it has settled down properly. Let the kitten explore its new home and do not try to rush it along. Avoid handling it too much during the first day – there will be plenty of time for cuddles later. Normally, it takes only a day or two for the kitten to settle down.

caring for
your exotic

Grooming and General Care

Perhaps one of the most appreciated aspects of the Exotic is that it does not require a great deal of grooming. However, the Exotic's dense, medium-length coat can tangle and become matted if not groomed properly, and you need to pay particular attention to the lower back and hips. Normally, one grooming session a week is ample, but when the cat is in moult, which happens once a year, usually in the summer, you may need to groom it every day, as a large amount of fur is shed. A moulted-out Exotic sheds most of its soft, woolly undercoat, which makes the coat appear thinner and lie flat. In this condition, the cat cannot win any shows, as this type of coat is totally the opposite to what the breed standard calls for. Most Exotics look like this during the hot summer months, and return to their usual dense coats once the weather turns colder.

To get through the cat's dense fur, you need a moulting comb, which has teeth of differing lengths. Comb through the cat's fur thoroughly. Once the comb moves through the fur easily, switch to a slicker brush and

From left to right: wide-toothed metal comb, fine-toothed metal comb, moulting comb, slicker brush and flea comb.

brush the coat. Some people advocate brushing the coat against its lay to ensure that it does not lie flat. This is not really necessary for a pet Exotic, but may be a good idea for a show cat. For both pet and show cats, powder grooming is very useful. Sprinkle a fine layer of unperfumed talcum powder all over the cat's coat, gently rubbing it into the fur with your fingers. Take care not to get any powder into the cat's eyes, nose or ears. Once the powder has been rubbed into the coat, brush it out again. This helps to condition the coat and remove the excess grease

Page 29 The Exotic's coat is dense and stands out from its body. Brylou Misty Lisa, bred by Louvane Stevenson, owned by John and Christine Wilson. Photograph by C. Wilson.

that makes the coat mat and lie flat. If you are grooming before a show, it is important to remember that no powder is allowed in the cat's coat during the show, so all traces must be removed beforehand.

If you find that the cat's coat starts getting matted more frequently than usual, or if it appears dirty, then it is time for a bath. Whether you use the bath, basin or a bowl, make sure that the cat has a non-slip surface to stand on, such as a rubber mat. The cat will panic if it slips in the water. Fill part of the bath or bowl with lukewarm water, and gently soak the coat through thoroughly (taking care to avoid nose, eyes and ears). Some people use a hand-held shower but, unless they have got used to it as a kitten, many cats forcefully disapprove of this. Once the coat is wet through, gently massage the shampoo into the coat. This should be a mild shampoo specifically manufactured for cats. Avoid dog shampoos, which can prove toxic to cats, and never use shampoos intended for adult humans beings. You can use baby shampoo as an alternative to cat shampoo. Next, every trace of shampoo must be rinsed out. Once the coat has been rinsed thoroughly, remove the cat from the water and rub its coat with a towel until it is as

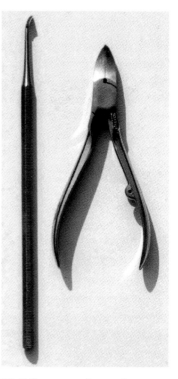

Nailclippers and a toothscraper are useful items for the Exotic owner.

dry as possible. If the cat will let you, finish the drying with a hairdryer. If not, put the cat in a warm room from which it cannot escape, where it has access to a radiator or fire. Soon the cat will settle down in front of the heat source and get dry. Once the coat is completely dry (and not before), comb it through carefully.

Normally your cat's ears should not need any attention. If there is a build-up of wax, a grey, greasy substance, wipe it away from the outer ear using a damp piece of cotton wool or special ear wipe available from pet shops and veterinary surgeries. Do not clean the inside of the ear, as this could create problems such as an excessive build-up of wax. If the ear appears dirty or smells bad, and if the cat is holding the ear down or actively scratching it, then see the vet.

Flat-faced cats such as the Exotic normally have a discharge from their eyes. This is nothing to worry about as long as it is either clear or brownish in colour, and the eye does not appear red, sore or swollen. Every day, gently wipe away any discharge from underneath and around the eyes using soft tissue, cotton wool or special eye wipes. Never touch the eye itself.

If your cat is allowed outdoors, then you should not trim its nails as it needs sharp claws to defend itself and to climb. If your cat is an indoor cat, you probably need to trim its claws regularly to minimise damage to your furniture and your hands. You have to trim the cat's claws before any show. Use human nail clippers or special cat claw cutters. Do not use cutters intended for dogs as

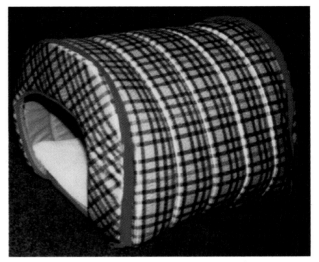
You can match the decor of your own home!

generally these are far too big, and snip off only the very tip of the claw. Trimming usually has to be done every two weeks or so, as the sharp tip of the claw regrows quickly.

Indoor or Outdoor Cat?

Whether your cat is kept indoors permanently or allowed outside needs careful consideration. Many people firmly believe that no cat can be happy if it is not allowed to go out, but this is not true, especially in the case of pedigree cats. Pedigree cats have been bred indoors for generations, so are well-adjusted to such a life. Some pedigree cats do not want to venture out, even if allowed. Others love to be able to go for a walk now and then.

Outdoor cats are subject to many risks, such as being run over, attacked by a dog, or getting into fights with other cats. There is also the chance that your cat simply disappears, something which does happen. Quite apart from this, there is the risk of disease. Illnesses such as Feline Leukaemia Virus (FeLV) and Feline Immunodeficiency Virus (FIV) are spread through saliva, mating and bites, so any outdoor cat that gets into a fight is at risk. These diseases are incurable and result in the cat's death. It is possible to vaccinate your cat against FeLV, but as yet there is no vaccine against FIV. An outdoor cat is also at greater risk from less serious ailments, such as earmites, fleas and viruses. Recent research carried out into the longevity of cats showed that outdoor cats live for an average of two years, whereas cats kept permanently indoors live for around 13 years.

If you do not want to keep your cat indoors all the time, yet are worried about the health risks, why not buy or build an enclosed run in your garden? That way your cat can spend some time outdoors without being put at risk. Some people enclose their entire back gardens! There are companies that manufacture and sell specialist cat houses and runs, or you may be able to make your own. Scan the cat magazines for advertisements.

It is no problem to keep the cat wholly indoors, as long as you make sure that you provide it with everything it needs. This incudes companionship (either in human or feline form), toys, a scratching post and a litter tray.

Vaccinations

All cats must be vaccinated against feline enteritis and feline influenza (Feline Rhinotracheitis and Feline Panleucopaenia, commonly known as cat flu). This should be done first at the age of approximately nine weeks, with a second injection three or four weeks later. The cat then needs a booster injection every year. Even indoor cats are at risk from these diseases, as the virus can be carried on the owner's clothing. It is vital to keep up with the vaccination programme. Nowadays it is also possible to vaccinate against other diseases, such as Feline Leukaemia. Exactly what is on offer and what is recommended, depends largely on whether you live in Great Britain or the United States. Ask your veterinary surgeon for advice. When you take your cat for its annual booster vaccinations, your vet will also give the cat a thorough check-up, making sure it is in good health.

A good quality cat carrier is essential.

Catbeds come in a variety of shapes and sizes.

Neutering

All cats not purchased specifically for breeding should be neutered. An un-neutered female comes into season (call) every two or three weeks during the warmer months, and sometimes during the entire year if kept indoors. When the queen is in call, she walks around howling like a banshee, looking for a mate. She may go off her food and might even start to urinate indoors. If not mated, she may develop fallopian cysts. An entire male has extremely strong-smelling urine, which more often than not he sprays all over his living quarters. He, too, calls loudly for a mate, and is not happy if not allowed access to females. If let out, he will get into fights and father unwanted kittens. A stud cat should be kept in his own, purpose-built cat house outdoors.

If they are neutered, however, none of these problems should occur, either in the male or female. The cat's temperament remains very much the same, except that the male's is often improved by neutering. It is an old wives' tale that neutered cats become fat and lazy. With the correct diet, and stimulating toys and company, neutered cats are no fatter or lazier than entire cats.

The best age to have your cat neutered is between six and ten months. Do not wait too long, as a male cat that has started to show behaviour such as spraying might not get out of the habit even when neutered. Neither should you have your cat neutered too early; make sure that it is of a good size first. Ask your vet for advice on when to neuter.

There is no need to let your female Exotic have a litter before she is neutered. It will do her no good at all; in fact, it may even make her pine for kittens for the rest of her life.

Equipment

You need certain equipment to care for your cat properly and keep it happy. There are numerous products on the market specifically manufactured for cats. Some are essential, such as a good quality cat carrier; others can be useful, such as the automatic cat feeding machine; others may be of little or no use. The following is a list of what you definitely need for your Exotic.

Food and Water Bowls Your cat needs one bowl for water and one for food. These should be easy to keep clean and unbreakable. Avoid plastic, as the surface scratches easily and bacteria can accumulate. Some cats have been known to have allergic reactions to the colouring of plastic bowls. The best bowls to use for both food and water are lightweight metal bowls, which come in many shapes and sizes.

Litter Tray This is absolutely essential for the indoor cat, but is useful for all cats, as they might need it during the night. Litter trays come in many shapes and sizes, and a large range of prices. Choose one that is not too small, offers your cat some privacy (with a hood) and is easy to keep clean. Place the litter tray in a quiet part of the house, not too close to where the cat is fed, as no cat likes to go to toilet near its feeding area. The cat litter is a matter of personal choice, as there are so many different types. There are earth-based litters in either grey or white, pellet-shaped litter consisting of compressed sawdust or paper, and many more. Some cats prefer one type over another, so it is often a case of trial and error until you find the type that suits you and your cat best. Remember always to keep the litter tray as clean as possible, as no

Disposable litter trays are now available.

cat likes to use a dirty toilet. If the litter tray is dirty, not only will it smell, but the cat may go to toilet elsewhere.

Combs and Brushes You need a metal moulting comb and a slicker brush (see Grooming, page 30). A flea comb may come in handy as it removes flea dirt and dead fleas effectively after treatment. However, it may be difficult to pull such a fine comb through the Exotic's dense coat.

Cat Carrier Never transport a cat in a cardboard box, as it can claw its way out if frightened. Cat carriers come in all sorts of different sizes and models. Choose one which opens at the top, as it is much easier to get your cat in and out than through a door at the side. The best type of cat carrier is made of tough plastic which is easy to clean, and has a door or lid of either the same material or metal. Make sure you choose a model that is big enough to offer plenty of room for your cat when adult; remember that Exotics grow to be quite big cats.

Nail Clippers Buy nail clippers intended for cats or for humans to keep your indoor cat's claws trimmed down. De-clawing, the surgical removal of the entire claw and the first toe joint, is not carried out in Great Britain. If you cannot stand the thought of your cat laddering your tights or scratching the furniture, then perhaps you should not have a cat in the first place. A cat without claws is a handicapped cat, as it cannot climb, jump and defend itself properly.

Scratching Post This is another essential for the indoor cat. Give your kitten a good-quality scratching post from the start and, hopefully, it will prefer to use this rather than your three-piece suite for claw exercise. If you delay buying a scratching post, your cat will use your furniture and carpet instead,

Scratching posts can be small, medium or large.

and this habit is almost impossible to break. Scratching posts come in an incredible array of shapes and sizes. Some are small boards covered in rope or carpet, others are elaborate climbing frames complete with play houses. The more interesting the post, the more likely your cat is to use it.

Toys All cats, especially kittens, enjoy toys. You can buy cat toys from pet shops, or simply let your cat play with a screwed-up piece of paper, a pine cone or an empty cotton reel. Everything is appreciated. Make sure that the cat cannot tear small pieces off the toy, which it may accidentally swallow. Especially popular toys tend to be the ones with the herb catnip added to them. These can be bought in pet shops, or you can make your own by stuffing an old baby sock with tissue, adding some catnip from the pet shop, and then stitching the sock so that it is securely closed.

Just one example of the variety of toys that you can find in your local pet shop.

Cat Bed A bed is not strictly necessary, but many cats appreciate having their own place to retire to, preferably on a raised surface as this is where cats like to sleep. Cat beds can take many different forms; choose the one that you think your cat will like. Don't expect it to use it all the time – if it decides to sleep on your armchair instead, there is not much you can do to stop it.

Collar and Disc If you let your cat go out, fit it with a collar and disc. The collar should be partly elasticated, so that the cat can wriggle out of it if it gets stuck. A reflective collar means that the cat can be seen in the dark. The disc should bear your name and phone number, and preferably the address as well. If you intend to show your cat do not let it wear a collar, as this marks the coat around the neck.

Golden Exotic kitten Moonwalkers Apache Gold.
The golden colour matures into a rich apricot.

feeding your
exotic

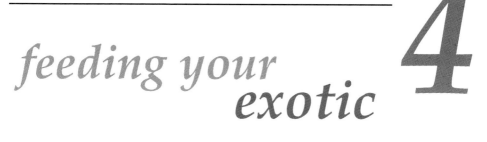

Feeding a cat is easy. You just open a tin from the supermarket, and that's it. No need to boil fish, or add vitamins or anything else to the cat's diet. Well, this is largely true nowadays, as there are so many excellent complete diets on the market. However, it is useful to have some knowledge of what a cat needs to thrive and stay healthy; if for no other reason than you will find it easier to choose the best food for your cat from among the bewildering number of brand names.

Kittens and adult cats have different requirements. A kitten needs twice as much protein as a fully-grown cat, so may fail to thrive if fed on a diet manufactured for adults. Older cats may require special diets, low in protein to protect failing kidneys, for example. These days, special diets are available for kittens, adults and older cats. If you are ever unsure how best to feed your cat, ask your vet for advice. Some specialist diets, such as kidney-friendly diets, are available only on prescription from veterinary surgeries.

How did cats survive before all these commercial diets? Years ago, the cat was an outdoor animal. When its body told it that it lacked protein, the cat went hunting; killing and eating birds, mice and rats, and so supplementing its diet quite well. This still works today for many feral cats, but a diet consisting mainly of birds and mice causes other problems, such as worms and parasites. Cats are unique in that they cannot survive without meat; they are obligate carnivores, unlike dogs which can survive on a completely vegetarian diet. An adult cat needs twice as much protein as an adult dog, and also needs certain nutrients that are not essential for the dog. Therefore, it is not advisable to feed your cat either on a home-made diet or on dog food, as the cat will develop deficiencies.

The Cat's Nutritional Requirements

The cat's intestine is adapted for a diet high in fat and protein, which means that it needs a diet high in energy but low in bulk. The cat needs proteins for tissue building, to be able to resist disease, for the maintenance of muscles and bones, and also to keep its coat in good condition. Proteins are made up of amino acids. To manufacture the protein, as many as 20 different amino acids are needed. Out of these, 10 can be manufactured by the body, but the other 10 must be gained through the diet. One of the best-known of these essential amino acids is taurine, which is present only in animal tissue. Without taurine, the cat cannot survive for any length of time. A taurine deficiency causes all sorts of problems, the most common being damaged eyesight and eventual blindness. Taurine deficiency can also cause brain damage, leading to death. Other problems include infertility, small litters, kittens that do not thrive and heart problems. This is the main reason

Page 39: Katy, a Shaded Silver, anticipates her supper.

Five-week-old kittens are ready to be weaned from their mother.

why it is absolutely essential not to feed your cat on dog food, as dogs are not dependent on taurine in the same way as cats. A dog can survive on cat food, but not vice versa.

The cat's body cannot manufacture some essential fats (fatty acids) so, again, these must be available through its food. Like protein, fats are used as a source of energy, and they help to prevent and conquer skin disease. One essential acid is arachidonic acid, which is present only in animal fats.

The cat does not actually require fibre, but a small amount in the diet may be useful. Fibre can help to get rid of furballs in the stomach, which develop when the cat swallows fur whilst grooming itself. It is also useful to help treat and prevent constipation. However, do not give too much fibre, or the cat is less able to digest its food. Excess water, that normally would have been disposed of through the kidneys, is retained in the intestines, which means that the urine becomes too concentrated. This in turn could lead to conditions such as Feline Urological Syndrome, a painful and potentially fatal condition (see chapter 8).

The cat does not need carbohydrates, such as cereal, but this is present in cheaper brands of cat food. A cat fed on a cheap food will not receive all the amino acids it requires.

Vitamins

Vitamins A and E are necessary for the functioning of the cat's membranes. Vitamin A is found only in animal tissue, reinforcing the fact that a cat needs meat to live. A deficiency of vitamin E will lead to painful inflammation in the cat's body. The group of B vitamins are needed by many different enzymes. Liver is a good source of both the A and B group of vitamins and is the main ingredient in many types of cat food, but do not give the cat fresh liver as this is addictive, and can cause problems if given for any length of time. The cat may develop vitamin A toxicity as a result. Thiamine, a B-vitamin, is very important for cats. Without this, a deficiency occurs which may result in brain damage. Fish contains an enzyme called thiaminase, which actually destroys thiamine. Because of this, any fish should be cooked so that this enzyme is destroyed. Vitamins K and D are important too; K for blood clotting and D is involved in bone metabolism.

Minerals

How much mineral the cat can absorb depends largely on what type of food it is being fed. If the diet is high in fat, then the absorption of calcium and trace elements is reduced. Calcium is important for bone formation, but can be harmful to growing kittens if too much is given, as it can actually retard growth. An excess of calcium can also reduce the absorption of certain other elements. On the other hand, too much phosphorus may result in a calcium deficiency and in kidney problems. Too much magnesium should be avoided as this can lead to Feline Urological Syndrome. Diets high in ash should avoided for the same reason, and sodium-rich diets may cause kidney problems too.

Choosing Your Cat's Diet

After all that, how do you choose a food for your cat? It may seem daunting at first, but is not that difficult; many excellent foods are available. First go to your kitten's breeder who can explain, preferably with a diet sheet, what the kitten has been fed on and what it should have in the future. Follow this advice, as breeders have a lot of experience of feeding growing kittens and adult cats. Another good source of advice is your vet.

Should you feed canned food, a complete dried food, or both? The main difference between canned and dry diets is the water content. All canned cat food contains at least 75% water. Dry food contains between 8 and 12% water and is therefore more economical, takes up less storage space, and the cat needs a smaller amount to gain all that it needs. However, if your cat is fed on only a complete dry diet, then it is essential that it drinks enough. Water is the cat's most important nutrient. Without water, the cat soon becomes dehydrated and dies; in fact, it will die from dehydration much sooner than from starvation. A cat given a canned diet automatically receives water through the food and you seldom, if ever, see a cat drink if it is fed this way, although fresh water should still always be available. Water is by far the best drink for adult cats, as milk should be given only to kittens, and possibly pregnant or lactating queens. Many adult cats, and pedigree cats in particular, are sensitive to cow's milk and develop diarrhoea if given it. You can buy from pet shops and supermarkets special cat milk that is less likely to cause problems, although this too can cause stomach upsets in a sensitive cat. Whether you feed a canned or dried diet is really up to you. Some owners opt to feed one type in the morning and the other in the evening, and there is nothing wrong with this.

It is a good idea always to read the label on the food packaging. The ingredients are listed in descending order of weight. In other words, the higher the place on the label, the more of that ingredient the food contains. It is worth remembering that meat and meat derivatives contain water, so may be heavier than, for instance, cereals, even if cereal is the main ingredient. Needless to say, the more specific the food manufacturer is about listing the ingredients of the diet, the easier it is to tell what quality that particular food is. A good-quality diet has mainly animal ingredients.

Feeding Your Adult Cat

An adult cat of nine months or over should receive two meals each day; one in the morning and one in the evening. The amount depends mainly on the quality of the diet; the cat needs more of a cheaper, cereal-based diet than of a higher-quality meat-based diet. Use your common sense, and do not necessarily follow the manufacturer's recommendation. An adult cat usually eats approximately a quarter of an average size can at each meal. Many cats like to feed on and off all day, nibbling at the food as the fancy takes them. The quality of canned food starts to deteriorate if it is kept at room temperature for too long, especially during hot weather. You can teach your cat to finish its meal in one go by removing its bowl once it has stopped eating, whether or not all the food is gone. If you keep more than one cat, probably they will finish the whole meal in one sitting to prevent somebody else from stealing it. Dry food can be left out all day.

Try not to spoil your cat, as this will only cause you problems in the future. Most cats have a preference for one food or another, and may refuse to eat a new

Blondbella Ballerina enjoying a good-quality moist food.

brand at first. If you give in and feed the cat only on what it wants, you effectively teach it that if it doesn't eat what's on offer, something better will soon appear. Some cats have trained their owners so well that they are only given one particular brand of cat food, or even just one flavour. Others refuse cat food altogether and live on leftovers or baby food, something which must be discouraged as the cat does not receive all that it needs. If your cat refuses to eat what you offer, remove the food and put down the same kind again at the next meal. Your cat will not starve itself to death, and will start to eat eventually.

Feeding Kittens

Feeding kittens is different from feeding adult cats, as kittens need twice as much protein and up to three times the energy than an adult cat. As kittens have such minute stomachs, their diet needs to be very concentrated. A kitten given a food intended for adult cats physically cannot eat as much food as it needs to gain all the essential nutrients. The kitten will fail to thrive and may become ill as its resistance to disease is lowered.

After weaning, your kitten needs to be fed on good quality kitten food in order to thrive.

Kittens up to the age of five or six months need four meals a day. One meal can then be dropped, and three meals given until the cat is adult at nine months of age. After this it can manage on two meals only. Obviously, if your kitten grows slowly and is not yet fully grown at the age of nine months, continue with three meals for a while longer.

Always feed a special kitten food. There are many excellent ones to choose from, both canned and dried. If a very young kitten refuses dry food, try soaking the food in water. Personally, I prefer to feed young kittens on a mixture of both: two meals of dry food a day, and two of canned food.

"Hey – dinner time!"

5

the exotic
show cat

What to Look For

Not all Exotics make show cats. Some may have too-long faces, others poor coat quality or a colouring fault. If you want to show your cat, tell the breeder when you buy your kitten. Do not pretend to yourself that your cheap pet kitten is a real bargain and that it will become a show winner. On the other hand, even if you have bought a kitten said to be of show quality, this is no guarantee of success on the show bench. The breeder can give you an opinion of the cat's quality at the point of sale. You cannot blame the breeder if the kitten later develops an undershot bite or poor eye colour, typical examples of faults that occur in adult cats. The area where you have the greatest influence is in the cat's adult size and condition. No matter how promising a kitten may be, if it is not fed and cared for correctly it will not grow up to be a good show specimen.

You should not accept any obvious faults in a kitten bought for showing. Any cat with a tail fault is heavily marked down at a show, and usually it is quite pointless to show it. Nor should it be bred from, as tail defects are hereditary. It should be perfectly possible to tell whether your kitten has a tail defect at the time of purchase. Similarly, a very badly undershot bite, possibly together with a twisted jaw, should be noticed by the breeder. A slightly undershot bite, on the other hand, may develop after the kitten has shed its milk teeth; this need not be a great problem as judges are often lenient in this respect. Kittens seldom show the coat colour that they will have as adults, so this is another area where true potential may be difficult to assess. However, if the kitten is marked, it should be possible to tell whether or not the markings are correct. Take care when choosing your potential show kitten, and do not be afraid to ask the breeder for advice. Most breeders are very honest and tell you about both good and bad points. It is also a good idea to read up on the breed standard (see page 100) before visiting the breeder, as this tells you in detail what an ideal Exotic should look like.

Head This should be round and large. The face is flat, without an overly long nose. The 'break', just above the kitten's nose, should be clearly defined. In the GCCF standard, it is considered a 'withholding fault' (judges are instructed to withhold certificates for adults or first prizes for kittens) if the upper edge of the nose leather is above the lower edge of the eye. This means that the cat should not be an 'ultra' or 'extreme' type Exotic. In such cats, the nose is situated right between the eyes, making the face very short and flat. There has been much controversy surrounding this rule (which also affects Persians) as some breeders prefer the ultra-type cat. However, it is still possible to have a very typy cat with

page 47: The Exotic's head should be round, with plenty of space between the ears. Owner and breeder: Christina Carpenter. Photograph by Alan Robinson.

Shaded Silver kitten, Hilal Katy, is an IC-winner.

a short nose without it becoming ultra. In the United States and many other countries, ultra is the norm and it is these cats that become champions. In Britain, ultras are found within the Exotic breed, but they are more common in the Persian. As the Exotic originally was bred from the British Shorthair, a too-long face is still a prevalent problem. A good face in an Exotic or a Persian is referred to as an 'open' face, which is the opposite of the ultra.

The cheeks need to be full and rounded. In some typy cats, you may feel a small dent on the cat's forehead just above the cat's eyes. Although some kittens may lose this indentation as they grow older and their bones develop, choose a kitten without such a fault. A skull indentation means that the cat may never be successful as a show cat, and there is also reason to believe that it is an inherited defect.

In an Exotic of good type, it should be possible to draw an imaginary vertical line from the cat's forehead across the nose and on to the chin. This is how flat the cat's profile should be, with a strong chin. An undershot bite is a common fault in flat-faced cats so do check the bite on your kitten. Ideally, the upper and lower teeth should be level with each other. In practice, this is seldom the case. A slightly undershot kitten may correct its bite once it has got its adult teeth, or it

A Redpoint Colourpointed Exotic of good type.
Photograph by Alan Robinson.

may not. Do not let such a kitten put you off if otherwise it is perfectly good, but avoid the kitten which is very clearly undershot, or has a jaw which is not perfectly aligned with the upper teeth.

The Exotic's ears should be well spaced, small and with rounded tips. Many Exotics' ears are far too large, which make them look

Under GCCF rules, all show equipment should be white.

unbalanced. The reason for this probably is that the Exotic's Persian ancestor also is required to have small ears but can disguise large ears in its quantity of fur. The Exotic has no fur to hide overlarge ears, so they are only too apparent. The ears should be fur covered on the inside, and they should not be 'open', which means that you should not be able to see straight into the cat's ears when viewing it from the front.

The eyes should be large and as round as possible; almond shaped or oval eyes are a fault. A good Exotic with a round, flat face and large, round eyes has the typical 'Teddybear' expression which is so appealing. Indeed, the Exotic is often known as the 'Teddybear cat', partly because of the face and eyes and partly because of the soft, plush fur. The colour of the eyes should correspond to the relevant colour standard, but all kittens are born with blue eyes and, even though the colour starts to change around eight weeks, it may take up to a year before the full eye colour has developed.

Body The Exotic should be medium or large in size, and most judges prefer them to be as large as possible. The cat should be heavy and cobby, with short, sturdy legs. Long, thin legs make the cat look unbalanced. The paws should be round and large. The tail is relatively short, but in proportion to the body. It should have a nicely-rounded tip and be free of any skeletal defects.

Coat The coat is the Exotic's special hallmark and is unlike the coat of any other breed of cat. It is longer than other shorthaired cats, but must not be long enough to flow. A too-long coat tends to lie flat and this is a fault. The coat should be so dense that it stands out from the body – you could compare it to a hedgehog with its prickles in a resting position. The coat should feel 'springy' and full of bounce.

Pr Erimicho Theolonius, a Brown Tabby, is quite relaxed in his show cage.
Owner: Jodie Page.

It should be soft, and lacks the harsher, crisp feel of the British Shorthair coat. Run your fingers through the cat's coat against the lay, and the coat will stay up for quite a while before slowly falling down into position again. If the coat falls back into place immediately, it is too short and not dense enough.

Types of Show

Within the GCCF, which licenses about 90% of all shows in Britain, there are three different categories of competition.

Exemption Show: This show is exempt from certain GCCF rules, hence the name. It is the first step on the ladder towards the Championship show, and is the first type of show that any cat club stages. No certificates or major prizes are on offer, and the classes may vary considerably. An Exemption show held by a breed club probably has plenty of different classes for all the colours of the breed. Exemption shows should be supported as, without a good attendance, the organising club cannot continue its climb towards obtaining a licence for a Championship show.

Some Exemption shows are held at agricultural shows or fetes, and are never intended to lead to anything higher. These shows are purely for fun. There are fewer classes than at most other shows, and probably no class specifically for Exotics. In this case, have a word with the show manager, who will probably let you enter your Exotic into one of the Persian classes. You will never make up a Champion by showing at Exemption shows, but they are usually small, very friendly, and an excellent starting point for the novice exhibitor. More experienced exhibitors enjoy them too, as there is no pressure to leave the show with a CC, so everyone can relax and enjoy the whole day.

Sanction Show: This is a dress rehearsal for the Championship show. The classes and rules are the same, but no certificates are on offer. A cat club needs to stage a number of Sanction shows before it is eligible to hold a Championship show. There are not many Sanction shows.

Championship Show: This is the most common show. Certificates are on offer which means that a good cat could be made up to, for example, Champion, Premier and Grand Champion. Championship shows are held nearly every weekend all over the country. They are organised by different cat clubs, each of which normally holds one Championship show a year. A Championship show can cover the following:

• all breeds, when it is usually organised by an area cat club, for example, the Yorkshire County Cat Club;

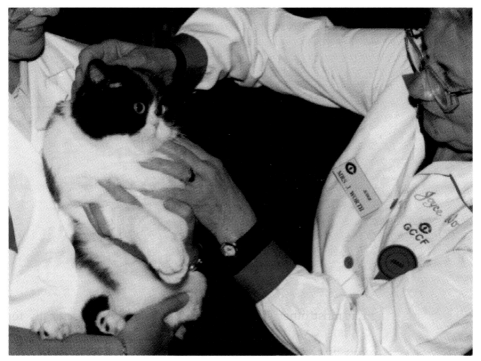

The steward holds the cat so that the judge can examine it closely.

• a breed group, which in the case of the Exotic would be the Longhair group. A breed group show may be organised either by a national club that covers the particular group, for example, the Longhair and Semi-Longhair Cat Club, or by an area club such as the North of Britain Longhair Cat Club;
• a single breed, organised by one of the breed clubs, such as the Exotic Cat Club. Championship shows can vary in size from around 50 to 150 cats in a breed show to over 1000 cats in an all-breed show.

The *Supreme Cat Show* is Britain's most prestigious cat show. This is the GCCF's annual show and can be described as a winner's show, or the feline equivalent of Crufts. The Supreme is a very large all-breed show, for which every cat has to qualify by winning at another Championship show. Kittens qualify by winning a first prize in an open breed class. Adults must have won at least one CC or PC. The Supreme Show is run differently from other GCCF shows, as the cats are taken to special rings to be judged, and their show pens can be decorated. The judges write down their comments, which are given to the exhibitor on the day. Some special certificates are on offer, which cannot be won at any other show.

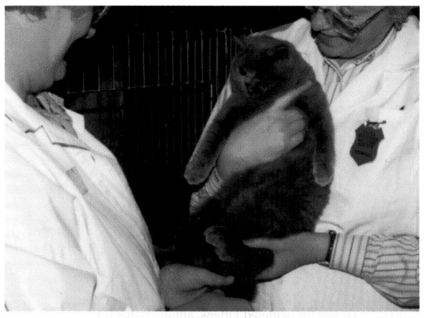

The judge examines the cat's tail for signs of any defects.

The *National Cat Club Show* is a very well-known show which, in close competition with the Supreme, is Britain's largest, with well over 1000 cats entered. This is another prestigious show and receives a lot of media attention. However, the National is just an ordinary Championship show, with no qualifications for entry and no special titles or certificates on offer.

Entering a Show

Registration and Transfer Before you enter your Exotic for a show, you must know with which body the cat is registered. In Britain there are two main registering bodies: the Governing Council of the Cat Fancy (GCCF) and the Cat Association of Great Britain (CA). The GCCF handles approximately 90% of all registrations. There are also some smaller organisations. If your cat is registered with the GCCF then you are not allowed to show it at a CA show, and vice versa. A GCCF rule states that no cat registered with them can be shown at non-GCCF affiliated shows, and any cat shown at a GCCF show must be registered with them.

Next, you must make sure that the cat has been transferred into your name. Any registered kitten is automatically listed as belonging to the breeder. The breeder should supply you with a transfer form, which must be signed by both of you, and your name and address entered. Send the form to the GCCF or CA together with the appropriate fee so the kitten can be transferred to you. You will be sent a new registration certificate (a transfer of ownership certificate) stating you are the owner of the cat. It is very important to remember that the cat must be registered in your name for you to be able to show it. You can enter your cat for a show if you have not had the transfer certificate through, but you must have sent it off no later than three weeks prior to the show. Also make sure that you enter the cat under the correct owner; for example, if you stated on the transfer form that your cat is owned by Mr and Mrs Smith, then the cat is registered as belonging to Mr and Mrs Smith and you cannot enter it as belonging only to Mr Smith.

Age There are strict rules as to the age when a kitten can be shown and, as these rules vary between the different organisations, it is important to find out all the relevant facts. The GCCF rules that a kitten must be no less than 14 weeks to be eligible for showing. A kitten is aged between 14 weeks and nine months. Once that cat has reached the age of nine calendar months (for example, a kitten born on 3 January becomes adult on 3 October) it counts as an adult. Any neutered cat can be shown only in the neuter classes. Normally neuters are adults, but some shows do offer classes for neutered kittens, although this is fairly rare.

Finding the Show Forthcoming shows are advertised in the magazines *Cat World* (a monthly publication where you can find adverts for both GCCF, CA and other shows) and *Cats* (the weekly journal of the GCCF). From the GCCF office you can obtain a show list that covers all shows during the show year, which runs from June to May. Having located a suitable show, send off for the schedule to the address advertised. Enclose a stamped addressed envelope of C5 size. It is important to send for your schedule well in advance as entries are closed approximately six weeks prior to the show. Most schedules are available three months prior to the show.

Show Information The schedule gives you all the information you need: what classes are on offer, who will be judging, entry fees, what time to arrive at the show, what prizes are on offer, and so on. It is important to check when the entries actually close. Most cat clubs can only accept a set number of cats into their show hall and, once this capacity has been reached, further entries have to be refused.

The sheer number of different classes on offer at Championship shows may seem bewildering at first, but a list in the schedule explains them. Exotics belong to the Longhair group so look at this section and find the open (breed) classes. Which open class you enter depends on the sex of your cat, and whether it is a kitten, an adult or a neuter. In the case of Exotics, two classes will be on offer for each category, one for males and one for females. At the moment all colours compete against each other in the same open class, but once numbers have risen significantly there is a good chance that the classes will be divided according to colour, as with Persians. You cat will be eligible only for one open class at any one show.

At GCCF shows, each cat must be entered into at least four classes, which normally means one open class and three (or more if you pay) miscellaneous classes, usually referred to as side classes. The relevant Exotic side classes will be listed under the Longhair heading. Your Exotic will probably have to compete against Persians in the side classes, as there are none specifically for Exotics except at breed shows. You will be able to enter your Exotic into any side class offered for Persians. The most common side classes are as follows:

Novice:	Exhibits that have not won a first prize in any class at a show held under GCCF rules.
Limit:	Exhibits that have not won more than four first prizes in any class at a show held under GCCF rules.
Debutante:	Exhibits that have never been shown at a show held under GCCF rules.
Maiden:	Exhibits that have not won a first, second or third prize in any class at a show held under GCCF rules.
Breeders:	Exhibits bred by owner.
Non-breeders:	Cat not bred by owner.
Junior:	Cat over nine months but under two years on the day of the show.
Senior:	Cat over two years old on the day of the show.
Adolescent:	Cat between nine and 15 calendar months on the day of the show.
Veteran:	Cat over seven years of age on the day of the show.
Aristocrat:	Cat that has won one or more CCs or PCs but is not yet a Champion or Premier.
Visitor:	Cat whose owner lives outside a defined area.
Radius:	Cat whose owner lives inside a defined area, usually a 35-mile radius of the show hall.

Most shows also offer club classes. These are sponsored by the club in question, and anybody wishing to enter must be a fully-paid-up member. The club classes also count as side classes and are listed after them in the schedule.

When entering your Exotic for the first time, I suggest that you enter the lowest classes, such as Debutante, Maiden and Novice. That way, your cat only competes against other (more or less) inexperienced cats. It is possible to enter

During judging at GCCF shows no-one, apart from the stewards and judges, is allowed in the hall.

more than three side classes – some shows have an unlimited entry, others let you enter a maximum of perhaps six classes, including the open. The obligatory three side classes are included in your entry fee, but anything above this incurs extra fees. I suggest that a cat going to its first show should enter only the minimum number of four classes. This means that the cat is handled four times (possibly by four different judges) and that is quite enough for any cat on its first outing. As your cat gains more experience, you can enter more classes if you wish.

The Entry Form When you have decided what classes to enter, it is time to fill in the entry form. This has to be completed identically to the cat's registration certificate. You need to fill in your name, address and phone number. The details required for the cat are: its registered name (exactly as printed on the registration certificate, not the cat's pet name), date of birth, registration number, breed number (this is on your Exotic's pedigree and on the registration certificate), sex

Once all the open classes have been judged, the exhibitors and general public are
allowed back into the show hall.

('M' for male, 'F' for female, 'MN' for male neuter, 'FN' for female neuter), the
cat's sire (including any titles the father may have), and dam (again including any
relevant titles), and the name of the breeder. If you bred the cat yourself, put
'exhibitor' in the column for 'breeder'. You then need to fill in the numbers of the
classes that you wish to enter. Write clearly, so that no mistakes can be made.
Finally, you need to sign the form and work out how much the entry is going to
cost you. Most clubs have a reduced fee for their members, so it may be worth
joining some clubs if you intend to continue to show.

Once the entry form has been correctly filled out, take a photocopy for your
own reference. If any mistake occurs in the show catalogue, this copy is your
proof of what you actually wrote down. You then need to check where to send

your entry; your Exotic entry needs to be sent to the Longhair section manager. Also check to see if you need to send a stamped addressed envelope with your entry. Most shows give out all the paperwork on the day, but some send it out in advance. In any case, it is a good idea to enclose a stamped addressed postcard so that the section manager can acknowledge receipt and acceptance of your entry. Finally, enclose your cheque or postal order for the correct entry fee.

The 13-day Rule

Within the GCCF, there is a regulation commonly known as the '13-day rule' (similar rules exist within many other bodies, although not all). This rule means that there must always be a clear 13 days between each show that you enter. You cannot enter two cats to two different shows a week apart – it is the household, not the cat, that is subject to the rule. In practice, this means that you can show cats every 14 days.

The rule exists to minimise the spread of disease and, in any case, to be shown once every 14 days is enough for any cat. A show will tire your cat out, and it deserves a rest between each outing. Some bodies, notably in America and on the continent, organise two-day shows, where the cats need to be present for both days. Personally, I feel that this is unfair on the cats.

Preparing for the Show

Being shorthaired, an Exotic does not need as extensive show preparation as a Persian, but it still must look its best on the day.

Bathing and Grooming Your Exotic may not need a bath before every show (as Persians certainly do), but if it has not been bathed for a while, has a coat that feels greasy or looks even the slightest bit dirty, then you should bath it. Judges pay a lot of attention to the cat's grooming, and a dirty and unkempt animal simply will not gain a high placing, no matter how good it is. You need to bath your Exotic approximately one week in advance, which ensures that some of the natural oils removed from the coat have a chance to return. A newly-bathed Exotic coat stands out in all directions, and does not look its best. Follow the bathing routine outlined in chapter 3. Once the cat is thoroughly dry, powder-groom it. Sprinkle a fine layer of baby powder all over the coat, and then brush it out again. Two days before the show, put more powder in the coat than you would normally. Gently rub it into the fur with your fingers, and then leave it for 24 hours. The day before the show, groom the cat really carefully, making sure every trace of powder is removed. If the judge see any powder on the cat, it will be disqualified. Blow hard into the coat to see if any powder is left.

When grooming your Exotic, brush the coat against the lay, to encourage it to stand out rather than lie flat. Take care not to upset your cat whilst doing this.

Guard Hairs You may find that your Exotic has long, coarse guard hairs distributed all over its body. Try to remove these by plucking them gently with your fingers, but do not pull out too many at a time as you will hurt the cat. The removal of these hairs enhances the cat's appearance, making the coat look tidier.

Ears Exotics are meant to have small, rounded ears but, as all cats have tufts of hair on the tips of their ears, its ears may appear to be pointed. Gently remove the tufts from the ear tips by pulling the hair out with your fingers – do not use scissors as this is too obvious and you want to achieve a natural look. Take care not to pluck too much fur or the cat will have a bald patch on its ear. Check the ears and wipe away any wax.

Nails The cat's claws need to be trimmed a day or two before the show (see page 32) so that it cannot scratch the judge or catch its claws on anything.

Ears The eyes must be clear and not weep too much. There should not be any staining around the eyes. You need to clean off the 'gutters' of brown staining underneath the eyes which show up clearly on pale coloured cats. If the stains have been left for some time, you may find that they have become more or less permanent. You can buy special 'tear stain removal' preparations from pet shops or trade stands at cat shows, which will bleach away the stains eventually, or use boric acid powder made into a paste and left on overnight. The best course of action is not to let any stains appear in the first place.

Coat and Skin Examine your cat's coat and skin carefully before you take it to the show. There must be no sign of fleas or flea dirt, or the cat will be rejected. Fleas are best eradicated with a good-quality flea spray, preferably purchased from your vet (see chapter 8). Remove any flea dirt or dead fleas with a flea comb. Exotics have such dense coats that it may be difficult to pull such a fine-toothed comb through the fur, but do persevere.

Next check your cat's skin. It must be pale and absolutely free of any scratches or lesions. It doesn't matter if you know that that small scratch is a result of a playful fight amongst your cats. If the vet finds any lesion, no matter how small, he will suspect ringworm and reject the animal. Any cat rejected for this reason will have to be examined by your own vet (together with any other cats that you own) and a clearance certificate sent to the GCCF before you can attend another show. It simply is not worth all that hassle for the sake of a small scrape, so always leave your cat at home if you find any scratch on its skin.

Proud owner/breeder Ruth Robertson with her Best in Show winning Tortie kitten, Ruuwen Pandora.

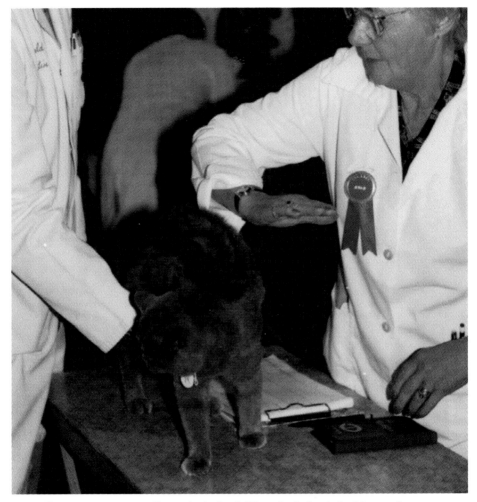

The cat is put on a trolley to be judged. Here the judge is looking at the coat.

Show Equipment What show equipment you need for your cat depends on whether or not it is a GCCF show. The CA and most other bodies let you decorate the cat's pen (in many cases, drapes are a requirement), as no judging takes place at the pens. With the GCCF, the judging takes place at the cats' pens, which must all look the same to keep the cats and their owners anonymous. The GCCF show pen is 60 x 60cm (24 x 24in) and must be furnished entirely in white: white blanket, white litter tray, and two white bowls – one for food and one for water.

The blanket must be plain with no distinguishing marks, and must not be cellular. Special show blankets can be bought at most shows. Green-backed veterinary bedding is allowed, which can be purchased from pet shops. Finding a white litter tray is not as easy as it sounds, as most are coloured, but the trade stands at cat shows sell them. Some pet shops offer a mail order service for complete 'show packs', and these usually advertise in the cat magazines. Choose a small litter tray as the space in the pen is limited. The food bowl can be any shape or size that you wish, as long as it is white. This is not allowed to remain in the pen whilst judging is in progress. The water bowl can be any shape, but the best type is semi-circular and hooks onto the side of the pen, as it is less like to be knocked over by the cat. The water bowl must be placed at the back of the show pen.

Most shows sell cat food and cat litter, but you may prefer to bring your own. You need the cat's up-to-date vaccination certificate, which may be required for inspection at vetting-in. All cats must have been vaccinated against cat flu and enteritis, usually no more than a year previously or less than a week before the show. Your cat's grooming equipment is also essential. Bring some tissue or cotton wool to wipe around your Exotic's eyes, in case they were weeping during the journey. You need a piece of narrow white ribbon or elastic to tie your cat's number tally around its neck. I find that elastic works best, as it can be tied into a makeshift collar which slips easily over the cat's neck.

Finally, all you need to bring to the show is your cat inside a secure carrier, yourself, the show schedule and your copy of the entry form.

The Show

Show days start early! GCCF shows open at around 8am, with judging taking place at 10am, so it probably means an early start for you and your cat. Do not feed your cat before you leave in case it is travel sick; you can feed it when you arrive at the show or after judging. Make sure that the cat travels as comfortably as possible, with a nice soft blanket in the carrier. Do not use the show blanket just in case the cat has an accident. Before putting your cat into the carrier, give it a quick groom and wipe away any tear stains. You will probably find a long queue ahead of you when you arrive at the show. First collect your cat's tally, vetting-in card and your exhibitor's ticket, if you have not received them already. The vetting-in card states all your cat's details as per your entry form.

Vetting-in You need the vetting-in card for the next step, the vetting-in. Vetting-in is a very thorough process and, no matter how many times you have been through it or how sure you are that your cat is perfectly healthy, it is still a nerve-wracking experience. When you reach the top of the queue, a steward directs you to a free table, where a vet and an assistant are waiting. Hand over your vetting-

Exotics generally have placid temperaments, making them ideal show cats.

in card, then get your cat out of the carrier for the examination. The vet will look at the cat's eyes, ears, mouth, coat and so on, checking for any sign of disease.

If your cat is rejected, the vet fills out a rejection form stating the reasons. There are several grades of rejection, ranging from A to D. Rejection under section A means that your cat is not allowed to take part in the show, and either you have to take it home or put it in an isolation pen for the rest of the day. A rejection under any of the other categories means that you cannot show that particular cat again (and sometimes no other cat from the same household) until you have provided the GCCF with a certificate from your own vet stating that the cat in question is perfectly healthy. Hopefully, this will never happen to you, and you need never go through the experience of being 'vetted out'! If your cat is in good condition and free of any parasites or skin lesions, then the vet signs your vetting-in card, and you can enter the show hall. Look after your vetting-in card as you may need it to collect prizes later in the day.

In the Hall Once inside the hall, find your cat's pen: the number is on the vetting-in card. Each row of pens has the numbers on both ends and each individual pen is numbered. All the kittens are penned together, all adults together and all neuters together, grouped by breed. Having found your pen, furnish it with your cat's blanket, litter tray and water bowl. Some people like to give the sides of the pen a quick wipe-down with some antiseptic before putting the cat in it. If it is a cold day, spread the blanket out to cover the entire pen. On a hot day, your cat will be more comfortable if you fold the blanket into a small square and place it in one corner. This way, the cat can choose whether it lies on the blanket or on the pen floor. If your cat considers the blanket too hot, it may simply decide to sit in its litter tray all day! The litter tray is normally placed at the left side of the pen, and the water bowl should be put at the back. Now is the time to feed your cat, as all food and food bowls must be removed by 10am when the judging starts.

Having sorted out the pen, give your cat a final grooming, put the tally around its neck and place the cat in the pen. Most cats settle down quickly, even if it is their first show. If your cat seems a bit uneasy, move away from the pen for a while so that it cannot see you. Check on it a few minutes later and, of course, always have a final look before judging starts.

Once your cat is settled, you can have a wander around the show. An announcement will be made just before judging starts, asking all exhibitors to leave the hall. Only the judges, stewards and officials are allowed inside the hall while the open classes are being judged. This is to make sure that there is plenty of space for them to move around, and also so that no judge can identify which cat belongs to which exhibitor. There is usually somewhere for the exhibitors to sit down, have a rest and enjoy some breakfast. In some halls you may be able to view the judging from a balcony, or from a roped-off area.

Another place to visit is the catalogue sales table. The catalogue lists each cat entered into the show by number, and gives all relevant details. The catalogue shows you how many entries there are in each of your cat's classes, and also gives lots of other information. Read it carefully and check that there are no mistakes regarding your cat. Any mistake, such as an incorrect class number or incorrect spelling needs to be reported to the show manager immediately. If the mistake was not yours (and this is where your copy of the entry form comes in handy) it can usually be rectified. If, on the other hand, you made the mistake, it depends on the severity whether or not it can be corrected. Serious mistakes may mean that your cat will be disqualified, so it is really important that you take great care when filling out your entry form.

Judging The judging now starts, and usually the open classes are judged first. These are the most important of all the classes. Each judge is allocated one steward, and they walk from pen to pen with a trolley. Each cat is judged on the trolley, which is wiped with disinfectant after inspection, as are the judge's and steward's hands. The cats are not actually scored on the points system (see page 101), which exists as a guide only. The steward notes down the judge's comments in the judging book, and the cats in each class are placed first, second and third according to the judge's opinion. The results are put up on the award board, where the exhibitors can check them. The award board lists only the number of the class, the pen numbers of the entered cats and the placings, so it is important to have your catalogue to hand when checking the results.

By about 1pm, the judging of the open classes has finished, the judges leave for lunch, and the exhibitors are allowed back in the hall. If you did not feed your cat when you arrived, now is the time to do so. Give your cat a cuddle and check that it is all right.

After lunch, those side classes that have not been judged are done, but this time the exhibitors are allowed to stay in the hall. Remember to keep out of the way, and never tell a judge that you are the owner of a particular cat, as this could lead to its disqualification. The side class results are displayed on the award board during the day, until all judging has finished.

If you have been lucky enough to win a trophy or rosette, check the procedure for receiving them. Most shows place rosettes for the open classes on the cats' pens, but expect you to collect any for side classes, as well as any trophies. There may be a choice of either rosettes or prize money for the side classes, although the money involved will be very small indeed!

Awards and Titles

There are various awards your Exotic can win. The highest your kitten can gain in the open class is a first prize and Best of Breed (BOB). The best of the two male and female class winners will be awarded the BOB, and usually receive a special rosette. Side classes can be quite large, with up to 20 entries in each class, so many shows award placings from first to sixth place. Others award the top three.

In adult open classes, first, second and third prizes are on offer, as well as a Challenge Certificate (CC). The CC is the all-important award that all exhibitors strive for. Three CCs awarded to your cat under three different judges make your cat a Champion. One CC is on offer for each of the Exotic adult open classes (male and female) and the best of the class winners is awarded BOB. The same applies for the neuter class, where the award is called the Premier Certificate (PC).

Once your cat has become either a Champion or a Premier, it can enter the

UK Grand Champion Owletts Maverick, the first Exotic Champion in Britain,
with owner Mike Clark.

Grand Champion (or Premier) class (sometimes referred to as Champion of
Champions and Premier of Premiers). These classes are restricted to titled cats,
and usually cover several breeds. Normally, there is one Grand class for Self
coloured Longhairs and one for Non-self coloured Longhairs. These two classes
are split into male and female. The winner of the Grand class may be awarded a
Grand Challenge Certificate (GCC, or 'Grand' for short), with the runner-up
awarded the Reserve Grand Challenge Certificate (RGCC). Neuters are awarded
Grand Premier Certificate (GPC) and Reserve Grand Premier Certificate (RGPC).

Three 'Grands' awarded under three different judges mean that the cat gains the title Grand Champion or Grand Premier. Once a cat has gained its title, the owner can choose whether to enter it into the relevant Grand class only, or into the ordinary open class as well. Any CC or PC awarded to a cat that already has its title does not count, and many people argue that it is unfair to show a made-up cat in the open class, as this may deny an un-titled cat the opportunity to win that all-important certificate. On the other hand, competition is much harder in the Grand classes, especially as the cat has to compete against other breeds, so many owners still want to show in the open. Personally, I believe that a titled cat should withdraw from the open class (the cat is still eligible to compete for BOB of the Exotics) but that is my opinion.

All of this may sound easy but, believe me, it is not. Judges are very strict, and they are instructed to withhold any award if the cat in question is not good enough or if it has any defect. If you show a cat with a tail defect, for example, then probably it will not be placed higher than second or third in the open class, even if it is the only entry for that class! The placing reflects the cat's quality, not the number of cats in the class. If the cat is not good enough, it will not win; it's as simple as that. This is most obvious in the adult and neuter open classes, where CCs and PCs are frequently withheld. Similarly, GCCs and GPCs may be withheld if the judge feels that none of the entered cats is of good enough quality to warrant becoming a Grand Champion or Premier. So, if your cat wins a first and a CC, even if it is the only cat entered, you know that it really deserves it.

If you have any queries about why your cat was placed in a particular way, you may approach the judge after all the classes are over. Otherwise, it is usually best to wait until the show report appears. This will be in *Cats*, the weekly magazine for exhibitors, and each show report normally appears about two to three months after the show.

Further titles can be won at the GCCF's Supreme Show. The overall winner of best adult and best neuter in show gains the title of Supreme Grand Champion or Premier respectively. The classes at the Supreme differ slightly from those at other Championship shows, being smaller and more split up, with no Champions or Premiers competing against un-titled cats.

If a Gr Ch or a Gr Pr wins its class and is deemed deserving of a certificate, then it is awarded a UK Grand Certificate (either CC or PC). Two UK Grands awarded under different judges make the cat a UK Grand Champion or Premier. It follows, therefore, that the highest title attained by any cat shown within the GCCF is Supreme UK Grand Champion or Premier. Very few cats go that far and as yet there are no Supreme Grands in the Exotic breed.

If your adult Champion or Grand Champion is then neutered, you have to start the whole process over again before you can win any Premier titles, as wins gained as an entire do not count when the cat is entered as a neuter. It is perfectly possible, if rare, to have a 'double titled' cat.

Close of the Show

Most cat shows close at 5pm. If you need to leave earlier for any reason, you have to ask for an early pass in advance from the show management. Quite a few shows do not issue early passes, as they need all the cats to be present when the general public is allowed in. An announcement is made when the show is officially closed, and you should not leave before this as it could result in your cat's awards being forfeited.

Showing Cats CA Style

The Cat Association of Britain is the British member of FIFe – the Fédération Internationale Féline. This means that all CA shows are run under FIFe conditions, which is the main style used on the continent.

All the pens at CA shows are 120 x 60cm (48 x 24in), double the size used at GCCF shows. As the judging does not take place at the pens, the owners are encouraged to decorate them. Each pen has some sort of floor covering and drapes. Each cat is taken to a judging ring (either by a steward or its owner) where the judge is seated at a table. Chairs are available so that the exhibitors can sit and watch the judging take place.

The cats are judged to a points system, and each cat is graded, such as 'excellent', 'very good', and so on. The awards also differ from GCCF awards, as do the titles. For a full list of classes, titles and show rules, contact the CA.

Showing Cats in America

Showing cats in the United States of America is slightly more complicated than in the United Kingdom, because there are no less than five major bodies which register cats and organise shows. The show rules, and even the standard of points, may vary between each body. Therefore, if you live in America, your best option is to get in touch with the different organisations, and ask for details of their show rules. To list every organisation's rules here would take up too much space. The cats themselves are of more extreme type, and the shows are organised differently. Each cat's pen must be decorated, and this is often done very lavishly. No vetting-in is required, and you may be allowed to use powders and sprays at the show to improve the cat's coat. Judging takes place in judging rings, and it is sometimes possible to show your cat in as many as four different judging rings at the same show. This means that your cat will be judged in four different breed classes (similar to the British open classes) and in theory could become a Champion at one single show. Titles are gained by collecting points from winning classes, and these are also calculated by how many other cats your cat has beaten.

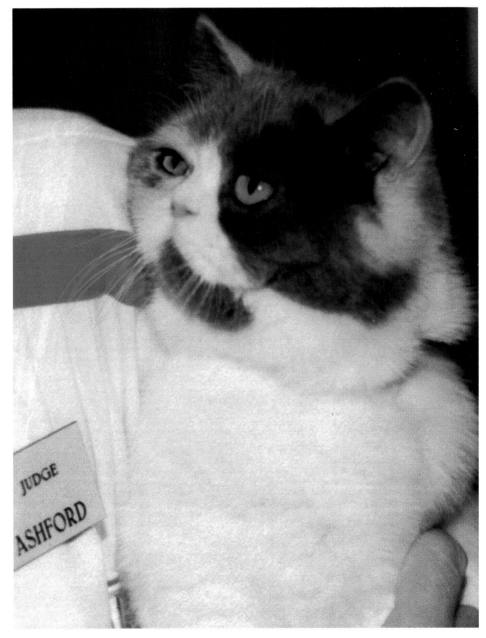

A Blue Tortie and White Exotic.

breeding
exotics

To Breed or Not to Breed

Cat breeding is a serious business, which you should not undertake lightly. Before breeding from your Exotic queen, ask yourself why you want to do this. Do you want to go through the experience of rearing a litter? Do you want to breed a kitten to keep back for yourself, either as a pet or show cat? Is it because you think that your queen needs to be bred from before being neutered? Or, perhaps, is it that you know Exotic kittens cost a lot to buy, and you would like to make some money out of your cat?

The first and second are good, honest reasons for wanting to breed a litter of kittens. If you want to breed for either of the other two, then I suggest that you forget the whole thing. A queen that is going to be neutered will not be any happier or healthier because she has been allowed one litter. In fact, it may have the opposite effect, as she may pine for kittens for the rest of her life. As for profiting from your cat, well, it may seem as though breeders make a lot of money, but this is the exception rather than the rule. There is a great deal of expense involved in rearing a litter, even before the kittens are born. If your queen has three kittens (the usual first litter size), and you decide to keep one kitten back for yourself, and at least one of the other two kittens is a Variant, then you will definitely make a loss. My first-ever litter of Exotics illustrates this point perfectly. The queen had to have a Caesarean, which naturally cost a lot of money – especially as it happened in the early hours of a Saturday morning, and the vet had to be called out. Only two kittens were born, and both turned out to be Variants. Not only that, both were male, so there was no possibility of using them for further breeding. I used to refer to these kittens as my 'chocolate teapots', as they were about as useful, and certainly they made a large hole in my pocket. However, they were adorable, and received the same amount of care and attention that they would have done had they been shorthaired or female.

Next, is your Exotic queen of good enough quality to breed from and is she on the active register? If your queen really is suitable only as a pet, then she is probably on the non-active list, and no kittens from such a queen can be registered. If your queen is not up to show standard, is it likely that she will have kittens of better quality than herself? Even if you want to keep a kitten back as a companion for the mother, you need to find homes for the rest of the litter, and this will be much more difficult if the kittens are not of show quality.

Another important question is whether the queen is healthy. Only breed from the healthiest cats, to avoid producing sickly kittens with defects. The queen needs to be in good condition overall, and must be of a good size. She should be

Page 73: Exotics can be mated successfully to Persians.
Shaded Silver Exotic Hilal Katy was mated to Golden Persian Ch Saraceeno Sundance.

neither too young nor too old. It is vital that she is blood tested before mating. No stud owner will accept your queen for mating if you have not got a certificate to prove that she has tested negative for Feline Leukemia Virus (FeLV) and Feline Immunodeficiency Virus (FIV). Some stud owners ask that your queen is tested for the presence of antibodies against Feline Infectious Peritonitis (FIP), although this is a less reliable test (see chapter 8).

Finally, have you got the time to spare to look after a pregnant queen and her kittens? The queen will probably care for her offspring with little or no help from you, but you do need to be available when the kittens are due, in case the mother needs assistance. It is no good going to work all day when your queen is due to litter; if she gets into trouble you may arrive home to find both her and kittens dead. You need to be with her until her litter is born. Should anything go wrong, you may need to hand rear the litter, which is a round-the-clock job for weeks. Also, you have to be on hand to help wean the kittens once they are old enough. Forget all the stray cats you see rearing their kittens by themselves. This is a pedigree cat I am talking about, and it is more sensitive. Also, do not forget that many strays lose their kittens, get ill themselves and frequently rear unhealthy kittens that never reach adulthood.

Finally, a word on economics. If you are lucky, you will get most of your outlay back once the kittens are sold, but you have to be prepared to spend a lot of money before this. There is the cost of blood testing your queen prior to mating, the cost of the journey to the stud, the stud fee, feeding the pregnant queen (she will need more food of a higher energy content), the cost of rearing the litter, registering and advertising your kittens for sale and there may be veterinary fees for the birth and vaccinations.

The Queen

Your queen should be mature and well grown before she is mated for the first time. A very large queen may be ready as young as ten months. Others are best left until they are 14–15 months old. If you are at all unsure, ask for advice from a more experienced breeder. The queen must not be too old, either. Most queens can be bred from safely until they are seven or eight years old, but a first litter, which puts more strain on the queen than subsequent ones, should arrive when the queen is between two and three years of age. Even if she is very fit (and a cat can hardly be called 'old' until it is at least ten years old), it can be harmful to the queen to come into season (call) time and time again before eventually she is mated. Neither is it a good idea to stop her from calling by a contraceptive pill or injections. These can cause problems such as womb infections and infertility, and may also result in deformed kittens.

These Persians show how the stud grabs the queen's neck during mating.

Selecting the Stud

One advantage of Exotics is that you have a choice in the mate for your queen: Exotic or Persian. The Exotic is still a comparatively rare breed, and there may not be any Exotic studs in your area. You should not hesitate to travel to have your queen mated, but it is better to avoid a very long journey for your queen's first mating, as it may put her off and stop her calling.

The most obvious reason for mating your queen to another Exotic is to reduce the number of Variant kittens in the litter. Virtually all Exotics carry the longhair gene, so will produce longhair kittens whether they are mated to another Exotic or to a Persian. Exotic x Exotic breedings will have to continue for several generations before the longhair gene is lost, and this is not done at the moment as outcrosses to Persians are needed to improve the Exotic type. In theory, an Exotic mated to a Persian should give you 50% Exotics and 50% Variants, but in practice you may have a litter of all Exotics or all Variants. When mating Exotic x Exotic, the likelihood of Exotic kittens is raised to 80% but, again, Variants can be produced.

You can also breed from a Variant queen. Most breeders sell all Variant kittens as pets, as breeding from these does not have any advantage over breeding from Exotics. However, if you have a female Variant of very good type and/or colour, you may want to breed from her all the same. She must be mated to an Exotic, not a Persian. Mating a Variant to a Persian means that all the resulting kittens will be longhaired, as the shorthair gene cannot be carried. A mating with an Exotic still produces some Variant kittens but, hopefully, some Exotics as well. Variant males are not used for breeding, because nobody wants to keep a Variant as a stud with all that this involves when they could keep an Exotic instead. British Shorthairs should not be used as this only ensures that a lot of the type is lost. It is still possible to breed a British Shorthair to a Persian and register the resulting offspring as Exotic, but this is not recommended as, again, a lot of type will be lost, and there really is no need as there are enough Exotics around.

Another important question is what colour to mate your Exotic queen to. As yet there are no restrictions regarding matings between various colours, so it is possible to 'mix and match' and create new colours. However, it is better to stick to matings where you know what colours will be produced. You need not mate your queen to a stud of the same colour; closely related colours will do just as well. For example, a Shaded Silver can be mated to another Shaded Silver, a Tipped or a Golden, with good results. A Blue can be mated to another Blue, a Cream, and a Red or a Black. A Blue-Cream or Tortie queen may be mated to a stud of either of those colours, and so on. It very much depends on what you want out of the mating. Colour genetics is a very complex subject, and much too large to be covered in this book. Read a specialist work and ask other breeders for advice. It is always advisable to find out beforehand what colours a particular mating can produce, so that you do not get any surprises once the litter is born.

Preferably the stud should not be too closely related to your queen (such as a brother, half brother or father), but some common ancestry is a good idea, as line breeding improves existing type and other desired qualities. Frequently, breeders find that kittens born from a line-bred litter are of better quality than kittens from a total outcross, where the queen and stud are unrelated. A good mating is, for example, cousin x cousin.

As far as possible, try to choose the stud to complement your queen. If she has a slightly-too-long face, choose a stud with a nice, short face. If she lacks in eye colour, the stud should

A sliding hatch separates the queen from the stud, but they can still see each other.

excel in this respect, and so on. Your aim is to produce kittens that are of better quality than their parents.

It goes without saying that you should choose a stud kept in good conditions and in good health. Just as the stud's owner will ask to see your queen's test certificates, you should ask for the stud's. If you do not like the conditions the stud is kept in, do not leave your queen there. A stud's quarters will always be rather smelly as an entire male has such strong-smelling urine, but the house and run should be clean and the stud in good condition. Longhaired studs such as Persians living in stud houses outdoors may not be as well groomed as your indoor queen, but at the same time they should not be heavily matted.

To find your stud, first find out if your breed club publishes a stud list. Some of the cat magazines list cats at stud, or you can talk to breeders at cat shows or approach the owner of a cat you like. Not all studs are at 'public stud'. 'Closed stud' means that the owners mate the stud only with their own queens, and no outsiders. Others are at 'limited stud', which means that the stud owner has certain conditions to be met before accepting a queen to stud. Usually, any limitations or conditions are mentioned in breeders' advertisements and stud lists.

The stud fee is decided by the stud's owner. How much this is depends upon the breed (Exotic studs usually command a higher fee than Persians), colour (rarer colours may cost more), and how good the stud is – a Champion's stud fee may be higher than an un-titled's, and a Grand Champion will probably cost more than a Champion. Check all the arrangements well in advance of the mating and get them in writing. When will the stud owner want the fee: before or after the mating has taken place? Will you get a free mating if your queen does not get pregnant? Will you be entitled to a free mating if your queen gives birth to only one kitten, or loses an entire litter? Most stud owners offer all this, but they have no obligation to do so, as the stud fee is the price you pay for the service, that is, the mating. Normally the stud fee is approximately half the price of a kitten. Some stud owners ask for a free kitten from the resulting litter.

Weighing the kitten will help you to monitor its condition.

Calling

Your queen will come into her first season between the ages of 10 and 18 months. Why the seasons are referred to as 'calling' soon becomes obvious! Behaviour varies between individual cats but, generally, a calling queen will do just that – call. She will miaow and howl, crying for a mate. She will roll around on the floor, and crouch down with her backside and tail pointing up in the air. If rubbed just above the tail, she will squirm and make noises somewhere between a purr and miaow. Some people, seeing a queen in call for the first time, think that she has injured herself and is in great pain.

Some queens, especially before they have had their first litter, do not make it obvious that they are calling. You may find that your queen only calls loudly when she is in a different room to you. Others have silent calls, with no other signs except that possibly they are more affectionate than usual. Such queens can be difficult to mate, as you do not know when to take her to stud. If this is the case, try to leave your queen with a stud for several weeks, as she will start calling at some point and, even if it is a silent call, the stud will notice and mate her. Any male cat, even a kitten or a neuter, may attempt to mount a calling queen, even though they are not fully capable of mating. Sometimes the first signs you notice of a queen being in call are tufts of fur which a male neuter has pulled out of her neck when attempting to mount her.

Cats that live outdoors usually only call and breed during the warmer months. Indoor queens can call at any time of the year, although your queen is still most receptive during the spring months. Once she has started calling, she does so regularly, with an average of three to four weeks between each call. If not mated, the queen will call more and more frequently, until eventually she may have a long, continuous call which does not finish until finally she is mated. When in call, she may go off her food, and it is not impossible that she will spray urine indoors. It is easy to see why it is important either to mate your queen or have her neutered; otherwise she becomes impossible to live with.

Mating

The optimum time to take the queen to stud is on the second or third day of her call. Most queens call for around five days. If brought to the stud too soon, the queen may go off call, put off by the journey and the unfamiliar surroundings. If you wait until she is well and truly in full call, the likelihood of her being mated successfully is much better. If you leave her for too long, she may go off call upon arrival in the stud's home.

Telephone the stud owner as soon as you notice any signs of your queen calling. Stud owners are people like everyone else, and it may be inconvenient if you turn up with just a few hours' notice. Do not forget to take all the relevant paperwork with you. Before you leave, make sure that your queen is in good health and free from fleas. If you do treat your queen for fleas, avoid any preparations that need to be applied to the cat's neck. The stud grabs the queen by the scruff during mating, and he may feel ill if he swallows flea killer. Do not be offended if the stud owner examines your queen on arrival, as he or she is only doing everything possible to ensure that the stud is kept healthy. Naturally, you should have wormed and vaccinated your queen before mating, as these procedures can be slightly dangerous to a pregnant queen.

The queen is not put in with the stud straight away. This may be dangerous, as the queen does not know the stud and may attack him. Most stud owners have separate queen's quarters, where she can be locked away from the male but they can see and smell each other. Once the cats have got used to each other, the stud owner will let the queen out under close supervision. If all is well, the cats can be left together to get on with things; if not, they may have to be kept separate for a while longer. Occasionally, a queen does not accept a stud and has to be held during mating, although this is a near impossible task, not to say dangerous for the person who is holding her! However, most Exotics are very good natured, and the queen happily accepts the stud. The pair are then left together for a few days, to mate at least twice. The first mating triggers ovulation, so the queen cannot become pregnant until the second mating. The stud owner keeps a close eye on the cats, and lets you know once a successful mating has taken place. This is usually recognised by the fact that the queen calls out, and may attack the stud as he withdraws from her because his penis is covered in small spikes. Once two or more matings have been observed, you can collect the queen. It is possible for a queen to give birth to a litter by two different fathers, so it is vital that she is kept away from other entire males for as long as she is in call.

Is the Queen Pregnant?

It takes about three weeks before you can tell whether the queen is pregnant. You may notice a subtle change as soon as you bring her home, such as an increased appetite, but this is by no means a sure sign. Three weeks after mating, a pregnant queen will 'pink up', which is a virtually foolproof signal. Her nipples increase in size considerably and take on a dark pink tinge. This is especially obvious in a maiden queen. If the queen has not pinked up after four weeks, probably she is not pregnant. If you are at all unsure, ask a veterinary surgeon to examine her approximately five weeks after mating.

The queen will not start calling again if she is pregnant. However, some queens have a short, 'false' call about six weeks after mating. If she has pinked up, you can disregard this call.

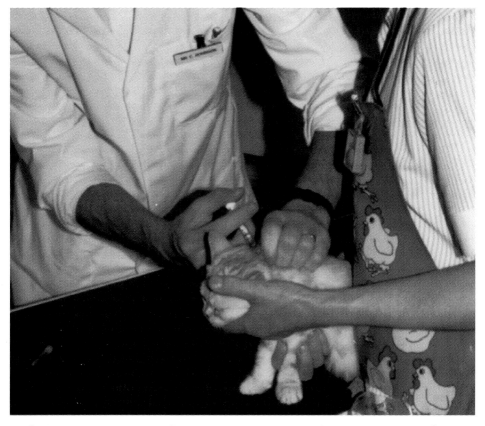

The kitten receives its second vaccination at 12 weeks, before it goes to its new home.

Caring for the Pregnant Queen

As soon as the queen's pregnancy is confirmed, start to treat her with more care than usual. Avoid handling her too much, do not use flea sprays unless you have to, and do not give any medication unless instructed by the vet.

Approximately five weeks into the pregnancy, give the queen three meals a day, and increase this to four as the pregnancy progresses. Make one or two meals of higher energy content than the usual diet; dry kitten food, for example, is excellent for pregnant queens. If kitten food is given, there is no need to add extra vitamins and minerals to the diet. If not, add a pinch of a supplement to the food every day – follow the manufacturer's instructions. If at all unsure, ask your vet for advice.

Milk is a useful supplement, as the extra calcium helps the queen to produce milk and also helps bone formation in the unborn kittens. Buy one of the special cat milks and, if she does not have any stomach upsets, give her a milk drink every day throughout her pregnancy. If she develops diarrhoea, she will have to make do with water. Some breeders give their queens a herbal supplement in the form of raspberry leaf (available from pet shops) from about the fifth week of pregnancy.

As the queen's due date approaches, introduce her to the kittening bed. This could be a cardboard box lined with old towels, or it could be a cat bed. Make sure that the sides of the bed are not so hard that a kitten is injured if the queen accidentally lies against it. Place the bed in a quiet spot in the house, preferably in your bedroom. Make sure no other cats or pets have access to it. If the queen is used to a kittening bed, she is far more likely to use it once her time comes rather than give birth under a bed or behind the furniture!

At five weeks, a Shaded Silver (left) and a Silver Tabby (right) still look alike.

The Birth

The gestation period is between 63 and 70 days, with most litters born after 65 days. Any litters born earlier than 63 days are premature, and problems may arise. If this happens, see a vet. There is nothing to worry about if your queen goes past 65 days, as long as she appears happy and in good health. Should she go past the 70th day without the kittens arriving, see a vet.

About the 60th day of pregnancy, confine the queen to one room. Make sure no other pets can get in and that the queen can get to her litter tray, food, water and the kittening bed. Place the bed in the most secluded corner to encourage her to use it. Most queens prefer to have as much privacy as possible when giving birth. If the kittening bed is in full view in the middle of the room, she may decide to give birth elsewhere – like one of my queens who gave birth underneath my baby's cot! Line the bed with a layer of old towels or blankets or, even better, a vet bed. A vet bed is warm and comfortable, and any wetness seeps through to the bottom layer, leaving the top dry. Make sure you have several, as you will need to change the bedding as soon as all the kittens are born, and afterwards at regular intervals.

Usually, the first sign that the queen is near to giving birth is that she goes off her food. If she refuses her evening meal, the chances are that her litter will be born during the night or the next morning. The second sign is 'nesting'; she tries to find a comfortable spot on her bed and rearranges her blankets. If she refuses to get into her bed, gently place her there. If she will not stay put, place the bed inside a kitten pen, as it is important that she gives birth in a safe place that you can get to easily.

Once the queen has finished nesting, she usually settles down and starts purring. Provided that she is quite placid and that you have a good relationship with her, she will be only too pleased for you to stay nearby and watch. As mentioned earlier, it is not advisable to let a queen give birth unsupervised, as complications can and do arise, in which case you need to be at hand.

When the queen's contractions start, her sides draw in for a few seconds and she may pant. Frequently a queen purrs during contractions, but in this instance purring is a sign of pain rather than contentment. The average amount of time between the first contraction and the birth of the first kitten is 30–60 minutes. If things continue for much longer than this, telephone your vet for advice, as the first kitten may be stuck. The first kitten is usually the most difficult one, and takes the longest time. Once one kitten has been born, the rest follow more easily.

Kittens are born either head first or feet first; both deliveries seem to be equally common. A true breech birth, when the bottom arrives first, is more rare and is likely to cause complications. Once part of a kitten can be seen, it should only take a couple of minutes until it is born. If not, you need to help it out.

Patrystar Cosworth is a British Blue male who has been used for Exotic breeding.
Owned by Pat Brice.

When it is born, the kitten is still enclosed in the amniotic sac. The queen breaks the sac and starts to clean the kitten, paying particular attention to the nostrils and mouth. Sometimes first-time mothers get slightly confused and break the sac elsewhere, neglecting to clear the kitten's nostrils and mouth. If this happens, break the sac yourself and get the kitten to breathe. Gently remove all the fluid from around the kitten's face with a towel or flannel. If it does not start to squeak, or is still lifeless, hold it upside down to drain the fluid from the lungs. Pinch its toes to encourage it to cry, which helps to clear the lungs. A healthy kitten should be pink around its nose, ears and feet. A blue tinge means that it is not getting enough oxygen. If needs be, hold the kitten firmly in one hand, support its head and swing it downwards. Use the towel to clear the nostrils and open the mouth and wipe away any fluid. The queen's vigorous washing helps to stimulate the kitten's blood circulation and breathing. If she fails to wash the kitten properly, imitate this action by rubbing it briskly with a towel.

One of the first things that the queen does is to chew off the umbilical cord and eat the attached placenta. Always check that each kitten is followed by the placenta so that you know it has not been retained inside the queen. If the queen lifts up the kitten when trying to break the cord, support it so that it does not develop an umbilical hernia. Some queens flatly refuse to chew the cord, in which case you have to break it yourself. Pull on it with your fingernails, approximately 2.5cm (1in) from the kitten's body. Pull towards the body, not away from it. You can also cut the cord with a pair of pre-sterilised scissors, but a clean break such as this is more likely to cause bleeding. If the queen does not eat the afterbirth, dispose of it yourself.

Once the kitten has been cleaned up and is breathing properly, it will start to make its way towards the queen's nipples for its first feed. By this time, the queen is about to give birth to the next kitten. The interval between each kitten is normally 20 to 30 minutes, although it can be as long as an hour. The most common size of a first litter is three or four kittens, although you can expect anything between one and six.

Weigh each kitten as it is born. Weight recording is important as it is the best way to tell whether a kitten is thriving. The usual birth weight is 90–120g (3–4oz), although smaller kittens are sometimes seen. A kitten weighing less than 60g (2oz) is not very likely to survive.

Once the queen has finished giving birth, she settles down to suckle her kittens. She will appreciate a feed and a drink herself. She will be reluctant to leave the kittens to start with, so you may have to feed her in bed, but be careful, as a bowl could topple over on top of a kitten. A suitable drink for the new mother is a mixture of special cat milk, an egg yolk and a teaspoon of glucose. This helps the queen get back some of her strength.

As soon as the queen leaves her kittens for the first time, change the bedding. Do this as quickly as possible, to avoid disturbing the queen or her kittens unnecessarily. Then leave the proud mother alone with her family. Do not bring lots of visitors to see the new arrivals, as this only distresses the queen and exposes the kittens to possible infections.

The stud house should incorporate a safety porch, so that visiting queens cannot escape.

Birthing Problems

Hopefully, your queen will give birth without any problems at all. It is, however, not uncommon for pedigree cats to need some sort of assistance, so it is important that you know what to look for.

The most common problem is a kitten getting stuck. This happens very frequently, especially if it is born with its hindlegs first. The tail, hindlegs and part of the body is visible but, despite the queen straining, the kitten does not move any further. If this happens, grasp the kitten in a firm but careful grip, preferably with your hand wrapped in a flannel or towel. With each contraction, pull the kitten outwards and downwards. Do not pull when the queen is resting between contractions, and take care not to grip or pull the kitten too hard. In most cases, you will find that the kitten suddenly slips out after a few pulls. If it is really stuck, try to make the queen stand up and move a few steps, as gravity helps to move the kitten out. Needless to say, if you find that a kitten is well and truly stuck, call your vet.

A kitten that has been stuck for some time before being born will be quite weak and may need some further assistance. The queen may be too tired to clean it and cut the cord. If the kitten isn't breathing, swing it in the air to clear the lungs, rub it vigorously and pinch its toes as outlined above. You can also give mouth-to-mouth resuscitation by very, very gently breathing into the kitten's mouth. Do not give up if the kitten appears lifeless at first; sometimes it may take as long as half an hour before it improves.

If your queen has been having contractions for over an hour, or if she has been straining for a long time after giving birth to one kitten, call the vet. There are many reasons why a queen fails to give birth naturally. A kitten may be stuck, or lying in such an awkward position that it cannot pass through the birth canal. Some queens have a too-narrow pelvis, in which case no kitten can pass through. If one kitten has taken a very long time to be born, the queen may be so exhausted that her contractions wear off and she cannot give birth to the rest of her litter. In all these cases, veterinary assistance is needed. Do not wait too long; vets do operate a 24-hour emergency service, and a queen in trouble is just such an emergency. She may need to have a kitten gently manipulated into position, she may need an injection of oxytocin to stimulate more contractions, or she may need a Caesarean. Caesareans are very safe these days, but ask your vet to use an anaesthetic from which your queen will recover quickly. If she is very groggy and disorientated as she wakes up, she may be unable or unwilling to care for her kittens. In this case you will need to hand rear the babies, at least until she is well enough to care for them herself.

If your queen has to have a Caesarean, it is important to find out why this has happened. If it was simply because a kitten was in the wrong position, or because the queen was exhausted after a difficult birth, there is no reason why this should happen again, and you can breed from her safely in the future. If, however, she failed to give birth naturally because of a narrow pelvis, she will have difficulties with every litter, and there is also the risk that any female kittens will inherit the same problem. In this case, the queen should not be bred from again, and your vet may be able to neuter her at the time of the Caesarean.

Deformed Kittens

Deformed kittens are, thankfully, comparatively rare. If your newborn kittens fail to thrive, suspect some form of deformity and take them to your vet. It is essential that you weigh the kittens regularly as this is the only sure way to tell whether they are thriving. A healthy kitten normally gains around 10g (0.35oz) every day from birth until it is a couple of weeks old, when the weight increase is even greater. It is a great cause for concern if a kitten fails to gain weight, or loses it.

First check that the kitten actually is suckling. Does it latch on to the queen's teat properly, and appear contented? A constantly-crying kitten, moving restlessly from nipple to nipple, may indicate that the queen is short of milk, or that the kitten has a cleft palate. In the first instance, you will have to supplement the kitten with a bottle – ask your vet for advice. A cleft palate occurs when the bones in the roof of the kitten's mouth fail to fuse properly, leaving a gap. Look at the roof of the kitten's mouth; there should be no visible slit or hole. A kitten with a cleft palate cannot drink normally and, even if bottlefed, fails to thrive as some of the milk inevitably ends up inside its lungs, causing pneumonia. The kitten should be put to sleep as soon as possible. The cause of cleft palates is not entirely known; it may be due to a deficiency in the queen, it may have been caused by the queen being given medication or exposed to pollution, or it may be hereditary.

Two other fairly common deformities are heart murmurs and twisted hindlegs. A kitten with a weak heart fails to thrive and may have a blue tinge to its nose and paws. A vet will be able to hear a murmur. This is caused by a hole in the heart which normally should have closed within hours of the birth. If this hasn't happened the heart will not work efficiently and, again, the kitten should be put to sleep to save it from suffering. Twisted hindlegs, or 'frog legs', appear to have been put on upside down. Some kittens can live despite this, although they need plenty of physiotherapy and exercise. How well they do depends on how severely the legs are affected and, again, your vet is the best judge of the condition.

The Kittens' Development

You will be amazed at how quickly the kittens develop. After only a day or so you can hear them purr as they suckle. Each kitten has its special nipple that it sticks to at all times. After a week, the kittens start to move around more and, when their eyes open at 6–12 days, they start to explore their bed. The opening eyes first show as small slits between the eyelids. The slit gradually increases over two or three days until the eyes are fully open. Do not force the eyes open. If there is a bit of brown discharge, gently wipe it away with a damp piece of cotton wool. If the eyes haven't opened after 14 days, gently bathe them with lukewarm water, as they could be damaged by staying closed for too long. The eyes are a deep blue when they first open, but change colour gradually from around the age of eight weeks.

At two weeks old, the kittens are walking around more confidently, and most start to climb out of their bed when they are three weeks old. To begin with, the queen carries them back immediately, but after a while she gives up as the kittens gain more confidence and do not stay put. At four weeks, the queen stops washing the kittens as much as she has done up until then, and no longer cleans

Four-week-old Blondbella Moonshine Magic has found a comfortable spot outside the kitten pen.

up their mess. The kittens start to use the litter tray, copying their mother. Make sure that the tray is low enough for them to climb into.

This is the age when you should start weaning the kittens. Their newly-cut teeth are very tiny, so start off with very soft food. Many breeders start weaning by mixing baby food (preferably chicken flavoured) with kitten milk, until it is nice and sloppy. Dip your finger into the mixture and offer it to the kitten. If it makes no attempt to lick your finger, open its mouth gently and put the mixture on to its tongue. No doubt it will look most offended but swallow the food. Continue like this until the kitten understands what to do. How long this takes varies between individual kittens. Some may eat baby food off a plate within five minutes, others may take a week! Once the kittens are eating the baby food, start feeding proper kittenfood, either canned or dry, or a mixture of both. If feeding canned food, mash it up thoroughly and make sure that it is served at room temperature. Keep the kittens' mother out of the way as she will have no scruples about stealing their food. Soak dry food in warm water to begin with to make it easier for the kittens to chew. Other suitable weaning foods are boiled fish and scrambled egg. Feed the kittens four or five times a day, and give them as much as they want at each meal. They will still suckle their mother, and should continue to do so for several weeks yet, so there is no need to offer a separate milk drink.

Take the kittens for their first injections and check-up when they are nine weeks old. The second injection is given when they are 12 weeks. By then, they are fairly independent (although some may still suckle their mother if she lets them) and probably the queen will be rather fed up with her maternal duties. A day or so after the second vaccination, the kittens can go to their new homes.

Exotics or Variants?

Unfortunately, there is no way that you can tell whether the kittens are Exotics or Variants until at least a couple of weeks after the birth. Then you can try to distinguish them by looking at their tails. Pull your fingers along the tail, from the tip towards the body to make the fur stand out. An Exotic kitten will have fur the same length all along the tail, whereas a Variant's fur is longer close to the base of the tail. This is not, however, a completely foolproof method. The fur of an Exotic feels harsher than that of a Variant, which is very soft. It is not easy to tell, and it is that much more difficult if your litter contains just Exotics or just Variants. However, after five or six weeks, there is no doubt as to your kittens' breeds.

Registering your Kittens

Carefully consider which register to put your kittens on. It is usually best to register any Variant kitten as non-active, which means that it cannot be bred from. As Variants are not eligible to be shown, this is also mentioned on the registration certificate. Any kitten that you feel may be good enough to breed from should be registered on the Active register. An Exotic kitten can still be shown if registered on the Non-active register, but cannot be bred from unless you, the breeder, apply for a transfer to the Active register and pay the appropriate fee.

Your kittens' names must also follow certain rules. Check these in advance with the registering body. Some bodies state that the kitten must have at least two words in its name, and the name must not be that of a famous living person or a place. There are usually restrictions on how many letters each kitten's name can include. A registered prefix (a sort of family name) will be put in front of each kitten's name. Contact your governing body for details on how to apply for a prefix.

Hilal Katy with her two newborn kittens.

Selling the Kittens

Disposing of your kittens is not simply a case of placing an advertisement in your local paper and selling the kittens to the first people willing to part with the money. Any responsible breeder takes every care to ensure that the kittens go to suitable homes, which includes 'vetting' potential buyers on their suitability as cat owners. Do not be afraid to refuse to sell a kitten to somebody that you do not like for one reason or another; your main priority must be to make sure that the kittens will be well cared for. The very best places to advertise are in the various cat magazines, in breed club journals and in show catalogues, as these are where genuine 'cat people' turn to when looking for a kitten.

Always sell the kitten directly to the person who is going to care for it. Breeders affiliated with the GCCF are not allowed to supply pet shops. Supply the purchaser with a pedigree, registration certificate, vaccination certificate, diet sheet and a sample of the food the kitten has been eating. Make sure you keep a note of the buyers' name, addresses and telephone numbers and encourage them to keep in touch. Always offer to help in any way that you can. I ask my buyers to sign a contract stating that the kitten has been sold for a specific purpose as this saves any confusion later. It also states that the breeder should be offered first refusal on having the kitten/cat back if it needs to be rehomed.

Whether it is your first litter or twenty-first, you will feel very sad to see your kittens go. Take heart from the fact that you have done all you possibly can to ensure they were raised properly and went to good homes.

Keeping a Stud Cat

Keeping a stud cat is not for the novice cat breeder. Within many cat clubs, there is an unwritten rule that a person should have been breeding regularly for at least five years before acquiring a stud. This is very sound advice. I have seen many novice breeders acquire a breeding queen and a stud at the same time. This simply is not practical, and usually ends with the stud being neutered or sold on. A maiden queen needs to be mated by a proven stud, and the inexperienced stud needs experienced queens on whom to practise his skills. It may work to put two inexperienced cats together, but if, for instance, the queen gets frightened and lashes out, the novice stud may be put off and be reluctant to mate other queens. Also, if the resulting litter has something wrong with it, or if no kittens are produced at all, it is useful to know that at least one of the cats has produced sound offspring earlier. That way, the breeder has a fair idea from which cat the problem stems.

To keep a stud if you have just one or two queens is simply not fair. A healthy, active stud needs a ready supply of queens or he becomes frustrated, lonely and bored. Most breeders solve this problem by letting other people use their stud, but this is difficult for the novice as it requires knowledge of breeding, mating, pregnancy, genetics, the rearing of kittens and so on – much of which can only be gained through experience. So, if you want to breed, go out to stud to start with.

If, on the other hand, you have been breeding for a few years and feel that now is the time to acquire your own stud, there are several things you need to look into carefully:

• Do you have enough queens to warrant keeping a stud? Ideally, you should have a minium of four queens to keep your stud happy and content.

• Do you have the facilities to keep a stud? An un-neutered male needs his own stud house outdoors with an attached run. Entire males frequently spray urine all over their living area to mark their territory. A stud kept indoors considers your house his territory so you can figure out the rest for yourself! Even if your stud does not spray, his urine smells very strongly and your house will smell. Finally, you do not want your queens to be mated indiscriminately, and you may have some you do not want to mate to this particular stud. Some queens may not show obvious signs of calling and then get mated without you realising that it has happened. Unless you put your queens on some form of contraceptive, it is virtually impossible to keep a stud and queens together unsupervised.

• Can you afford to buy and keep a stud? A good-quality male cat, especially a proven adult, is not cheap, and a good-quality stud house is also expensive.

If the answers to the above are yes, now to find a suitable cat. Your best option is to buy an adult that is already proven, that is, has sired kittens with good results. That way, you know that you are getting a stud capable of doing the work you want him for. Most breeders opt for a kitten, which is more risky as you do not know how he will turn out. With any luck, your kitten will grow into a nice looking adult with no serious fault and, once old enough, can be put to the test with an experienced queen. Most males show an interest in mating around the age of 10 months, although some are slower and may be over a year old before they start working.

Naturally your stud should be a suitable colour to complement your queens; I do not recommend that you mix colours too different in their genetic make-up. Whether you buy an Exotic or a Persian is up to you. With an Exotic you may end up with more Exotic kittens; but with a Persian you may find a cat of better type, have a wider choice of cats to buy, and also be able to accept Persian queens.

Study your stud's pedigree carefully. You do not want a stud that is closely related to your queens, but a more distant relative from the same breeding lines is usually a very good thing. Also check the pedigree for the colours and breeds

Littermates Milagro Bonita (left) and Milagro Bambino, Blue Exotics bred and owned by Christina Carpenter. Photograph by A. Robinson.

it includes. Certain colours, notably self Blues, are best kept pure, that is, there should only be Blues in the pedigrees, or possibly Blue, Cream and Blue-Cream. Some colours can be carried, and it is important that you know the pedigrees of your cats well and have some grasp of genetics so that you know what colour kittens are likely to be produced.

The stud house is an important purchase. An adult stud needs to go straight out into his house although a kitten can stay indoors until he matures. You can either buy one out of a variety of houses from a specialist cat house company or build one yourself. Whichever method you choose, bear these points in mind:

• The size of the house and run. The stud will live in the house probably all his life so he is entitled to some space. Many cat houses are far too small. Exotics and Persians are large cats and need a fair amount of space. As a guideline, give your cat a house at least 180 x 90cm (6 x 3ft) with a run of no less than 180 x 270cm (6 x 9ft). The larger the stud house, the better.

• You need separate queen's quarters inside the house. This can take the form of either a partition within the house, or a large holding pen.
• Especially if you are going to accept other people's queens for stud, you must make sure that the house and run are secure and that the cats cannot escape. Fit all doors with bolts and padlocks, and the outer door should have a safety porch in front.

• What sort of weather protection your stud house and run have depends on where you live; in temperate climates you should certainly consider putting a roof over the run, partially-boarding runs, insulating the actual house and adding some form of rain protection.

• Your stud should have shelves to sleep on and to climb, good scratching posts and/or cat trees, a comfortable warm bed, toys, a litter tray and food and water bowls. The windows should be either shatterproof or fitted with wire. For dark winter evenings, an electric light in the run is a must, and an infrared light heater fitted to the ceiling may also be a good idea. However, Exotics and Persians have heavy, dense coats and do not need as much extra heat as shortcoated coats.

• The house and run need to be easy to clean, especially as your stud may spray the walls.

So now you have your stud safely installed in his new quarters. You will soon find that he calls almost as much as a queen (which may not be too popular with your neighbours) and he does this because he wants a mate. Before letting him have a queen for the first time, make sure that both cats are blood tested, and that their vaccinations are up to date, even if both belong to you. The GCCF requires a Certificate of Entirety before you can register any kittens from your stud. Contact the GCCF for a form, which you need to take to your vet with your cat. The vet will confirm that the stud has two normal testicles.

If your stud is familiar with your queen from living with her as a kitten, you can probably leave the two cats together to get on with their business. If not, close supervision is essential so that neither cat gets injured. Obviously, the same applies to visiting queens; both queen and stud must be supervised. Before you can offer your cat at public stud, he must have proved himself by siring a litter. Then you can advertise his services in the various cat magazines, and put him on the breed clubs' stud lists.

To keep a stud means lots of hard work. He must not be forgotten out in his house, and must have plenty of visits from you with time for grooming and cuddles. But when your first litter, sired by your own stud, is born, you will realise that all the effort is very worthwhile.

colour varieties **7**
of the exotic

The Exotic is available in many colour varieties, and more are being developed. Some are more popular than others, and therefore seen in greater numbers. Some of the most popular colours include the Self (all one colour), Blue and Cream, Blue-Cream, Shaded Silver and Colourpoint (which has markings like the Colourpoint Persian, also known as Himalayan). A full list of all the colour varieties recognised by the GCCF in Britain appears opposite.

The breed number preceding the name is a code that tells what colour and breed the cat is. Exotic is breed

Patrystar Confetti, a Blue and White Tortie, owned, bred and photographed by Pat Brice.

number 70, so all Exotic breed numbers begin with 70. The following number describes the cat's colour or markings, so 70:16 stands for Blue Exotic, 70:40 for Colourpointed Exotic. If the cat is marked in any way, then a third number or letter is added; for example, Bluepoint Colourpointed Exotic is breed number 70:40:2. Apart from the addition of the 70, the Exotic's breed numbers are identical to those used by British Shorthairs.

Once you have learnt your breed numbers, it is quite easy to work out what colour a particular cat is. In pedigrees, the cat's name is often followed by the breed number and registration number, with no further information given. A GCCF booklet lists every breed number for every GCCF-recognised breed. I have chosen to list the GCCF breed numbers and standards because the GCCF is the oldest registering body in the world, and by far the largest one in Britain. However, other registering bodies may use different breed numbers, and may have slightly different standards, particularly in the United States.

Page 97: A Brown Tabby Exotic, photographed by Alan Robinson.

EXOTIC COLOUR VARIETIES

70:14	Blue Eyed White	70:30d	Red Spotted Tabby
70:14a	Orange Eyed White	70:30s	Silver Spotted
70:14b	Odd Eyed White	70:31	Black and White Bi-colour
70:15	Black	70:31a	Blue and White Bi-colour
70:15b	Chocolate	70:31b	Chocolate and White Bi-colour
70:15c	Lilac	70:31c	Lilac and White Bi-colour
70:15d	Red Self	70:31d	Red and White Bi-colour
70:16	Blue	70:31f	Cream and White Bi-colour
70:17	Cream	70:31w	Black and White Van Pattern
70:18	Silver Tabby	70:31aw	Blue and White Van Pattern
70:19	Red Tabby	70:31bw	Chocolate and White Van Pattern
70:20	Brown Tabby		
70:20a	Blue Tabby	70:31cw	Lilac and White Van Pattern
70:20b	Chocolate Tabby	70:31dw	Red and White Van Pattern
70:20c	Lilac Tabby	70:31fw	Cream and White Van Pattern
70:20e	Tortie Tabby	70:36	Black Smoke
70:20g	Blue Tabby	70:36a	Blue Smoke
70:20h	Chocolate Tortie Tabby	70:36b	Chocolate Smoke
70:20j	Lilac Tortie Tabby	70:36c	Lilac Smoke
70:21	Tortoiseshell	70:36d	Red Smoke
70:21b	Chocolate Tortoiseshell	70:36e	Tortie Smoke
70:21c	Lilac Tortie	70:36f	Cream Smoke
70:22	Tortie and White	70:36h	Chocolate Tortie Smoke
70:22a	Blue Tortie and White	70:36j	Lilac Tortie Smoke
70:22b	Chocolate Tortie and White	70:39	Black Tipped
70:22c	Lilac Tortie and White	70:39d	Red Tipped
70:22w	Tortie and White Van Pattern	70:39f	Cream Tipped
70:22aw	Blue Tortie and White Van Pattern	70:40:1	SealPoint Colourpoint
		70:40:2	BluePoint Colourpoint
70:22bw	Chocolate Tortie and White Van Pattern	70:40:3	ChocolatePoint Colourpoint
		70:40:4	LilacPoint Colourpoint
70:22cw	Lilac Tortie andWhite Van Pattern	70:40:5	RedPoint Colourpoint
		70:40:6	SealTortie Point Colourpoint
70:28	Blue-Cream	70:40:7	CreamPoint Colourpoint
70:30	Brown Spotted Tabby	70:40:8	Blue-CreamPoint Colourpoint
70:30a	Blue Sotted Tabby	70:40:9	Chocolate TortiePoint Colourpoint
70:30b	Chocolate Spotted Tabby		
70:30c	Lilac Spotted Tabby	70:40:10	Lilac-CreamPoint Colourpoint

70:40:12	Blue TabbyPoint Colourpoint	70:40:11	Seal TabbyPoint Colourpoint
70:40:13	Chocolate TabbyPoint Colourpoint	70:40:20	Lilac-Cream TabbyPoint Colourpoint
70:40:14	Lilac TabbyPoint Colourpoint	70:73	Pewter
70:40:15	RedTabbyPoint Colourpoint	70:73a	Blue Pewter
70:40:16	Seal Tortie TabbyPoint Colourpoint	70:74	Golden
		70:75	Shaded Silver
70:40:17	Cream TabbyPoint Colourpoint	70:75a	Blue Shaded Silver
		70:75d	Red Shaded Silver
70:40:18	Blue-Cream TabbyPoint Colourpoint	70:75e	Tortie Shaded Silver
		70:75f	Cream Shaded Silver
70:40:19	Chocolate Tortie TabbyPoint Colourpoint	70:75g	Blue-Cream Shaded Silver

THE BREED STANDARD

Every recognised breed of cat has a written breed standard. This describes in detail what an ideal example of the breed should look like regarding body shape, coat quality and so on. In addition, every colour variety of each breed has a colour standard. The following is the complete breed standard for the Exotic reproduced by kind permission of the GCCF.

General Type Standard

Head and Ears: Head round and massive with good breadth of skull; well balanced. Small round-tipped ears, set wide apart and low on the head, fitting into the rounded contour of the head, not unduly open at the base. Full cheeks; round forehead. Short broad nose of even width with stop (break). Nose leather fully formed. Strong chin and full muzzle with broad and powerful jaws, without a 'pinch'. Short thick neck.

Eyes: Large full round eyes; brilliant in colour and set well apart. Bold and not deep set.

Body: Large or medium in size; of cobby type; low on the legs. Broad deep chest; massive shoulders and rump; well rounded.

Legs and Paws: Short thick strong legs. Large round firm paws, toes carried close: five in front, four behind.

Tail: Short, but in proportion to the body length.

Coat: Dense, plush, soft in texture, full of life; stands out from body due to density, not flat or close-lying. Medium in length, slightly longer than other Shorthairs but not long enough to flow.

The Blue-Cream, as its name suggests, should show a mixture of both Blue and Cream, as in Cyntander Annie's Song, owned by Christina Carpenter.
Photograph by C Carpenter

Scale of Points

Head: including size and shape of eyes, ear shape and set.................................30
Body: including shape, size, bone,legs and paws, and length of tail...................20
Coat..20
Colour...20
Eye colour 10
Total 100

Withhold Certificates or First Prizes in Kitten Open Classes for:
1   The upper edge of the nose leather above the lower edge of the eye.
2   Any defect as listed in the Standards of Points booklet.

Faults
1   Orange ring in green-eyed cats.
2   Green ring in orange-eyed cats.

SELF EXOTIC

Blue-eyed White Exotic (70:14)
Colour: Pure white, free of marks or shade of any kind. Nose leather, eye rims and paw pads pink.
Note: White kittens sometimes have some coloured hairs on the head and should not be penalised for this.
Eyes: Decidedly blue, deeper shades preferred.

Orange-eyed White Exotic (70:14a)
Colour: As for Blue-eyed White Exotic.
Eyes: Copper or deep orange.

Odd-eyed White Exotic (70:14b)
Colour: As for Blue-eyed White Exotic.
Eyes: One eye blue and one eye orange or deep copper.

Black Exotic (70:15)
Colour: Lustrous dense black, sound and even in colour, free from rustiness, shading, markings or white hairs. Nose leather, eye rims and paw pads black.
Note: Black kittens often show grey or rusting in their coat; this should not be unduly penalised.
Eyes: Copper or deep orange.

Chocolate Exotic (70:15b)
Colour: Medium to dark chocolate, warm in tone, sound and even in colour, free from shading, markings or white hairs. Nose leather, eye rims, pads chocolate.
Note: Chocolate kittens sometimes show greying in their coat and should not be unduly penalised for this.
Eyes: Copper or deep orange.

Lilac Exotic (70:15c)
Colour: Lilac, warm in tone and sound and even in colour, free from shading, markings and white hairs. Nose leather, eye rims and paw pads lilac.
Eyes: Copper or deep orange.

Red-Self Exotic (70:15d)
Colour: Deep rich red, free of white hairs, sound and even in colour, coat to be as free of markings as possible: ghost tail rings may be visible, slight shading on the forehead and legs is acceptable. Nose leather, eye rims and paw pads pink.
Eyes: Copper or deep orange.

Blue Exotic (70:16)
Colour: Medium to pale blue, sound and even in colour, free of shading, markings or white hairs. Nose leather, eye rims and paw pads blue-grey.
Eyes: Copper or deep orange.

Cream Exotic (70:17)
Colour: Pale to medium cream, sound and even in colour without a white undercoat; coat to be as free of markings as possible: ghost tail rings may be visible. Nose leather, eye rims and paw pads pink.
Eyes: Copper or deep orange.

Additional Withholding Faults for all Self Exotics:
1 White lockets, spots or tip to tail.
2 Tabby markings (see Red Self and Cream).
3 Incorrect or extremely pale eye colour.
4 Flecks or traces of incorrect colour in either iris.
5 Incorrect pigment in nose leather, eye rims or paw pads.
6 Almond or oriental eye shape and/or set.

TABBY EXOTIC

Classic Tabby Pattern
All markings should be clearly defined and dense. On the forehead there should be a letter 'M' giving the impression of a frown. There should be an unbroken stripe running back from the outer corner of the eye and narrow lines on the cheeks. On the neck and upper chest there should be unbroken necklaces, the more the better. The edges of the ears to be the same colour as the markings with a central patch of ground colour resembling a thumb print. A series of lines run from above the 'M' marking over the top of the head and extend to the shoulder markings. The shoulder markings form the outline of a butterfly, when viewed from above. Both upper and lower 'wings' should be clearly defined with the central areas broken by small areas of ground colour. On the back there should be an unbroken line running down the spine from the butterfly to the tail, with a stripe running parallel on either side of this. These stripes should be separated

Milagro Bambino, Blue, and Milagro Bendito, Cream.

Bred by Christina Carpenter. Photograph by C Carpenter.

from each other by stripes of ground colour. On each flank there should be an 'oyster-shaped' patch, surrounded by one or more unbroken rings. The tail should have complete rings, as numerous as possible, with the tip of the tail being the same colour as the markings. The legs should be barred evenly with bracelets from the body markings to the toes which are spotted. The abdominal region should also be spotted. Ground colour and markings should be evenly balanced and both sides of the cat should have identical markings.

Mackerel Tabby Pattern
The Mackerel Tabby Pattern differs from the Classic Tabby Pattern only in the body markings. A narrow unbroken central spine line is flanked on either side by a broken spine line from which the narrow lines which form the Mackerel pattern run vertically down the body; these lines should be as narrow and numerous as possible. The tail rings, again as narrow and numerous as possible, may be complete or broken with the tip of the tail being the same colour as the markings.

Silver Tabby Exotic (70:18)
Ground Colour: Silver in all areas including chin and lips.
Markings: Dense black.
Eyes: Green or hazel.
Nose Leather: Brick red preferred, though black is permissible.
Pads and Feet: Paw pads black. Black markings on the hind legs extending (when adult) from the soles of the feet, up the back of the leg, to the hock joint.

Additional Faults:
1 Brown tinge on nose or paws. 2 Pale, brindled or uneven ground colour.

Red Tabby Exotic (70:19)
Ground Colour: Red in all areas, including chin and lips.
Markings: Deep rich red.
Eyes: Deep orange or copper.
Nose Leather: Brick red.
Pads and Feet: Paw pads red. Red markings on the hind legs extending (when adult) from the soles of the feet, up the back of the leg, to the hock joint.

Additional Fault: Pale, brindled or uneven ground colour.

Brown Tabby Exotic (70:20)
Ground Colour: Rich, copper brown in all areas, including chin and lips.
Markings: Dense black.
Eyes: Copper, orange or deep gold.

Red Tabby Exotic, photographed by Alan Robinson.

Nose Leather: Brick red preferred, though black is permissible.
Pads and Feet: Paw pads black. Black markings on the hind legs extending (when adult) from the soles of the feet, up the back of the leg, to the hock joint.

Additional Fault: Pale, brindled or uneven ground colour.

Blue Tabby Exotic (70:20a)
Ground Colour: Cool-toned beige in all areas.
Markings: Deep blue affording a good contrast with ground colour.
Eyes: Copper, orange or deep gold.
Nose Leather and Paw Pads: Blue or pink.

Additional Fault: Brindling in ground colour or markings.

Chocolate Tabby Exotic (70:20b)
Ground Colour: A warm-toned bronze ground of agouti hairs.
Markings: Rich chocolate brown.
Eyes: Copper, orange or deep gold.
Nose Leather: Chocolate or pink rimmed with chocolate.
Eye Rims and Paw Pads: Chocolate.

Additional Fault: Brindling in ground colour or markings.

Lilac Tabby Exotic (70:20c)
Ground Colour: Cool-toned beige in all areas.
Markings: Lilac.
Eyes: Copper, orange or deep gold.
Nose Leather: Lilac or pink rimmed with lilac.
Eye Rims and Paw Pads: Lilac.

Additional Fault: Brindling in ground colour or markings.

Cream Tabby Exotic (70:20f)
Ground Colour: Pale-toned cream in all areas, including chin and lips.
Markings: Rich cream affording a contrast with ground colour.
Eyes: Copper, deep orange.
Nose Leather and Paw Pads: Pink.

Additional Fault: Brindling in ground colour or markings.

Additional Withholding Faults for all Tabby Exotics:
1 Serious pattern faults.

2 White anywhere.
3 Incorrect eye colour or rims or flecks of contrasting colour (in adults).

TORTIE TABBY EXOTIC

A Tabby cat in which the tabby pattern is overlaid with shades of red or cream. Both elements, tabby and tortie, must be clearly visible.

Tortie Tabby Exotic (70:20e)
Colour: The base Tabby pattern should consist of dense black markings on a brilliant copper brown agouti background with shades of red.
Eyes: Copper, orange or deep gold.
Nose Leather: Brick red and/or pink.
Paw Pads: Black and/or pink, depending on the distribution of the red.

Blue Tortie Tabby Exotic (70:20g)
Colour: The base Tabby pattern should consist of deep blue markings on a cool-toned beige agouti background overlaid with shades of cream.
Eyes: Copper, orange or deep gold.
Nose Leather: Blue and/or pink.
Paw Pads: Blue and/or pink depending on the distribution of the cream.

Chocolate Tortie Tabby Exotic (70:20h)
Colour: The base Tabby pattern should consist of rich chocolate markings on a bronze agouti background overlaid with shades of red.
Eyes: Copper, orange or deep gold.
Nose Leather: Chocolate and/or pink.
Paw Pads: Chocolate and/or pink depending on the distribution of the red.

Lilac Tortie Tabby Exotic (70:20j)
Colour: The base Tabby pattern should consist of lilac markings on a beige agouti back ground which has been overlaid with shades of cream.
Eyes: Copper, orange or deep gold.
Nose Leather: Faded lilac and/or pink.
Paw Pads: Faded lilac and/or pink depending on the distribution of the cream.

Additional Withholding Faults for all Tortie Tabby Exotic:
1 Serious pattern faults.
2 White anywhere.
3 Incorrect eye colour or rims or flecks of contrasting eye colour (in adults).

TORTIE EXOTIC

Tortie Exotic (70:21)
Colour: Black and shades of red, intermingled – all feet and the tail to be broken with colour. Small patches of colour need not penalise an otherwise good exhibit; a blaze on the face is permissible.
Eyes: Copper, orange or deep gold.
Nose Leather and Paw Pads: Pink and/or black.

Additional Fault: Tabby markings (in adults).

Chocolate Tortie Exotic (70:21b)
Colour: Chocolate, light red and dark red, intermingled – all feet and the tail to be broken with colour. Small patches of colour need not penalise an otherwise good exhibit.
Eyes: Copper, orange or deep gold.
Nose Leather and Paw Pads: Chocolate and/or pink.

Additional Fault: Tabby markings (in adults).

Lilac-Cream Exotic (70:21c)
Colour: Lilac and shades of cream, softly intermingled – all feet and the tail to be broken with colour.
Eyes: Copper, orange or deep gold.
Nose Leather and Paw Pads: Faded lilac and/or pink.

Additional Fault: Tabby markings (in adults).

Additional Withholding Faults for all Tortie Exotics:
1   White anywhere.
2   Incorrect eye colour or rings or flecks of contrasting eye colour (in adults).

TORTIE AND WHITE EXOTIC

Tortie and White Exotic (70:22)
Colour: Three colours, black and shades of red, to be well distributed and broken and interspersed with white, at least one-third and not more than one-half the coat.
Eyes: Copper, orange or deep gold.
Nose Leather and Paw Pads: Black and/or pink.

Ch Vivaldi Virtuoso, a Seal Tabbypoint Colourpointed Exotic.
Bred by Wendy Wallace.

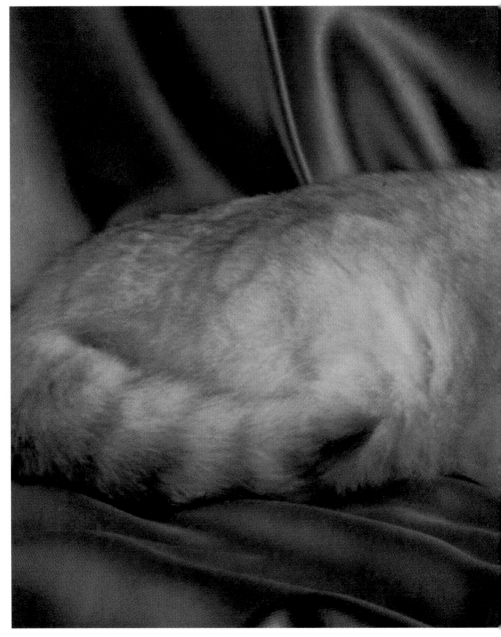

The Tipped Exotic is a shade lighter than the Shaded Silver.

Photograph by Alan Robinson.

Blue Tortie and White Exotic (70:22a)
Colour: Patches of light to medium blue, pale-toned cream and white to be well distributed and broken. The white to be at least one-third and not more than one-half the coat.
Eyes: Copper, orange or deep gold.
Nose Leather and Paw Pads: Blue and/or pink.

A Golden Exotic kitten.

Chocolate Tortie and White Exotic (70:22b)
Colour: Patches of chocolate, light red and dark red to be well distributed and interspersed with white. The white to be at least one-third and not more than one-half the coat.
Eyes: Copper, orange or deep gold.
Nose Leather and Paw Pads: Chocolate and/or pink.

Lilac Tortie and White Exotic (70:22c)
Colour: Patches of lilac and shades of cream to be well distributed and broken and inter-spersed with white. The white to be at least one-third and not more than one-half the coat.
Eyes: Copper, orange or deep gold.
Nose Leather and Paw Pads: Faded lilac and/or pink.

Additional Withholding Faults for all Tortie and White Exotic:
1 A predominance of white.
2 Incorrect eye colour or rings or flecks of contrasting eye colour (in adults).

Additional Faults for all Tortie and White Exotic:
1 Tabby markings.
2 Brindling or white hairs in the coloured patches.
3 Incorrect proportion of any colour.

Blue-Cream Exotic (70:28)
Colour: Blue and cream softly intermingled. All feet and the tail to be broken with colour. Small patches of colour need not penalise an otherwise good exhibit. A blaze on the face is permissible.
Eyes: Copper, orange or deep gold.
Nose Leather and Paw Pads: Blue and/or pink.

Additional Withholding Faults:
1 White anywhere.
2 Unsound coat.
3 Incorrect eye colour or rings or flecks of contrasting eye colour (in adults).

Additional Faults:
1 Uneven balance of colour.
2 Colour unbroken on paws.
3 Brindling.
4 Tabby markings.
5 Silver tipping (in adults).

SPOTTED TABBY EXOTIC

All markings to be clearly defined and dense. On the forehead a letter 'M' gives the impression of a frown. An unbroken stripe should run back from the outer corner of the eye and narrow lines on the cheeks. A series of lines run from above the 'M' markings, over the top of the head and extend to the shoulder markings. On the neck and upper chest there should be unbroken necklaces, the more the better. The edges of the ears to be the same colour as the markings with a central patch of ground colour resembling a thumb print.

The pattern on the body and legs should consist of numerous well-defined, oval, round or rosette-shaped spots which follow the Tabby pattern in distribution. The tail should have numerous narrow rings or spots, the tip of the tail being the same colour as the markings.

Brown Spotted Tabby Exotic (70:30)
Colour: Dense black spotting on a warm-toned coppery brown ground of agouti hairs.
Eyes: Copper, orange or deep gold.
Nose Leather: Brick preferred though black is permissible.
Paw Pads: Black.

Blue Spotted Tabby Exotic (70:30a)
Colour: Light to medium blue spotting on a cool-toned beige ground of agouti hairs.
Eyes: Copper, orange or deep gold.
Nose Leather and Paw Pads: Blue or pink.

Chocolate Spotted Tabby Exotic (70:30b)
Colour: Rich warm-toned chocolate brown spotting on a warm-toned bronze ground of agouti hairs.
Eyes: Copper, orange or deep gold.
Nose Leather: Chocolate or pink rimmed with chocolate.
Paw Pads: Chocolate.

Lilac Spotted Tabby Exotic (70:30c)
Colour: Lilac spotting on a cool-toned beige ground of agouti hairs.
Eyes: Copper, orange or deep gold.
Nose Leather: Lilac or pink rimmed with lilac.

Red Spotted Tabby Exotic (70:30d)
Colour: Rich warm-toned red spotting on a ground of bright apricot hairs.
Eyes: Copper, orange or deep gold.
Nose Leather: Brick red.
Paw Pads: Red.

Cream Spotted Tabby Exotic (70:30f)
Colour: Rich cream spotting on a cool-toned paler cream ground.
Eyes: Copper, orange or deep gold.
Nose Leather and Paw Pads: Pink.

Additional Withholding Faults for all Spotted Tabby Exotics:
1 Serious pattern faults.   2 White anywhere.
3 Incorrect eye colour or rings or flecks of contrasting eye colour (in adults).

Additional Faults for all Spotted Tabby Exotic:
1 Brindling or uneven ground colour.
2 Unbroken spine line, linked spots or bars.

Silver Spotted Tabby Exotic (70:30s)
Colour: Dense black spotting on a silver ground of agouti hairs.
Eyes: Green or hazel.
Nose Leather: Brick red preferred though black is permissible.
Paw Pads: Black.

Brown Spotted Exotic. Photograph by Alan Robinson

Additional Faults:
1 Brown tinge on nose or paws.
2 Pale, brindled or uneven ground colour.
3 Solid black, linked spots, bars.

Bi-Colour Exotic (70:31–70:31f)
Colour: Solid colour and white, the patches of colour to be clear, even and well distributed. Not more than two-thirds of the cat's coat to be coloured and not more than one-half to be white. Face to be patched with colour and white.
Eyes: Copper, orange or deep gold.
Nose Leather and Paw Pads: Pink and/or the colour corresponding to the colour of the patches.

Additional Withholding Faults:
1 Tabby markings.
2 Brindling or white hairs in the coloured patches.
3 Incorrect proportion of white.

Van Distribution Bi-colour and Tri-colour Exotic
(70:31w–70:31fw and 70:22w– 70:22fw)
The coat should be basically white with the colour confined to the head, ears and tail. For perfection, no colour on the body or legs, but up to three small 'spots' of colour are allowed in an otherwise excellent example of the breed. The coloured areas need not be a uniform shape and, whilst the markings should preferably show a visual balance, symmetry is not essential. Tail to be fully coloured.

Smoke Exotic (70:36–70:36j)
Colour: A Smoke is a cat of contrasts, darker on back, head and feet. Any colour accepted in the recognised Exotic, the undercoat being as white as possible, showing maximum contrast. No tabby markings in adults, but kittens should not be penalised too heavily.
Eyes: Copper, orange or deep gold.
Nose Leather and Paw Pads: Corresponding with coat colour.

Additional Withholding Faults:
1 Tabby markings.
2 White or silver guard hairs.
3 Insufficient contrast.

Tipped Exotic (70:39–70:39j)
Colour: Tipping to be of any colour accepted in the recognised Longhair breeds.

The undercoat to be as white as possible. Coat on the back, flanks, head, ears and tail to be tipped with colour. This tipping to be evenly distributed thus giving the characteristic sparkling appearance. The legs may be very slightly shaded with tipping, but the chin, stomach, chest and underside of tail must be pure white. Any tabby markings to be considered a defect. The visible skin on the rims of the eyes to correspond with coat colour.

Eyes: Cats with black tipping: emerald green or blue-green. All other colours: copper, orange or deep gold.

Nose Leather: Cats with black tipping: brick red. All other colours: to correspond with coat colour.

Paw Pads: Cats with black tipping: black or seal. All other colours: to correspond with coat colour.

Additional Withholding Fault: Incorrect eye colour or rims or flecks of contrasting colour (in adults).

Additional Faults:
1 Barring on legs.
2 Tabby markings with the exception of ghost tail rings which should not penalise an otherwise good exhibit.

COLOURPOINTED EXOTIC

There should be a good contrast between the points and body colour. Light body shading, if present, to be confined to the shoulders and flanks, and should tone with the points. The points (mask, legs, feet and tail) should be as evenly coloured as possible. The mask should cover the entire face, including the chin and whisker pads; it should not extend over the head, although the mask of a mature male is more extensive than a mature female. The points should be free of white hairs and any areas of non-pigmented fur. Eye colour to be pure and decidedly blue.
Note: The rate at which points colour develops in all Colourpointed Exotics is variable, the dilute colours taking the longest.

Solid Pointed Colours
The colour on all points should be evenly matched in tone and free from any sign of patchiness. Nose leather, eye rims and paw pads to tone with points colour.

Seal Colourpointed Exotic (70:40:1)
Points seal brown with toning creamy-white body colour.

Blue Colourpointed Exotic (70:40:2)
Points blue with glacial white body colour.

Chocolate Colourpointed Exotic (70:40:3)
Points chocolate in colour and warm in tone, with ivory-white body colour.

Lilac Colourpointed Exotic (70:40:4)
Points lilac in colour and warm in tone with magnolia-white body colour.

Red Colourpointed Exotic (70:40:5)
Points rich red with apricot-white body colour.

Cream Colourpointed Exotic (70:40:7)
Points cream with toning creamy-white body colour.

Tortie Smoke, one of the rarer colours.

Tortie Point Colours
The colour on the points should be the base seal, blue, chocolate or lilac, which has been broken with shades of red or cream. Ideally, all points should show some red or cream. A blaze is permissible. Nose leather, eye rims and paw pads to tone with the points colour.

Seal Tortie Colourpointed Exotic (70:40:6)
Points seal broken with shades of red; toning creamy body colour.

Blue-Cream Colourpointed Exotic (70:40:8)
Points blue and shades of cream; glacial to creamy-white body colour.

ChocolateTortie Colourpointed Exotic (70:40:9)
Points chocolate and shades of red; ivory to apricot-white body colour.

Lilac-Cream Colourpointed Exotic (70:40:10)
Points lilac and shades of cream; magnolia to creamy-white body colour.

The Shaded Silver should have a pure white chest and underside.
Photograph by Alan Robinson.

TABBY COLOURPOINTED

There should be a clearly defined 'M' marking on the forehead, 'spectacle' markings round the eyes and spotted whisker pads. The front legs have broken rings from the toes upwards; barring on the hind legs is confined to the front of the upper leg and thigh, the back of the leg from toe to hock being solid points colour. Ears solid but showing clear 'thumb marks' which are less apparent in dilute colours and mottled in the Tortie Tabbypoints. Hair inside the ears lighter, giving the appearance of a pale rim; tail rings. Nose leather pinkish outlined in pigment, or to tone with the points. Eye rims and paw pads to tone with the points.

Non-Tortie Tabby Colourpointed
These colours show distinct tabby markings, but are much more subtle in dilute colours.

Seal Tabbypointed Exotic (70:40:11)
Seal brown markings on a pale brown agouti background; body colour a toning creamy-white. Nose fur may be ginger towards the leather.

BlueTabbypointed Exotic (70:40:12)
Blue markings on a light beige agouti background; body colour glacial white. Nose fur may be fawn towards the leather.

Chocolate Tabbypointed Exotic (70:40:13)
Chocolate markings on a light bronze agouti background; body colour ivory-white. Nose fur may be bronze towards the leather.

Lilac Tabbypointed Exotic (70:40:14)
Lilac markings on a pale beige agouti background; body colour magnolia-white.

Red Tabbypointed Exotic (70:40:15)
Rich red markings on a light apricot agouti background; body colour apricot-white.

Cream Tabbypointed Exotic (70:40:17)
Cream markings on a paler cream agouti background; body colour a toning creamy-white.

Tortie Tabby Pointed
These colours show the normal tabby pattern which has been overlaid with

shades of red or cream. The extent and distribution of the tortie areas is not important providing that both elements, tortie and tabby, are clearly visible.

Seal Tortie Tabbypointed Exotic (70:40:16)
Seal brown markings on a pale brown agouti background; overlaid and patched with shades of red; toning creamy body colour.

Blue-Cream Tabbypointed Exotic (70:40:18)
Blue markings on a light beige agouti background; overlaid and patched with shades of cream; body colour glacial to creamy-white.

Chocolate Tortie Tabbypointed Exotic (70:40:19)
Chocolate markings on a light bronze agouti background; overlaid and patched with shades of red; body colour ivory to apricot-white.

Lilac-Cream Tabbypointed Exotic (70:40:20)
Lilac markings on a pale beige agouti background; overlaid with shades of cream, body colour magnolia to creamy-white.

Additional Withholding Faults for all Colourpointed Exotics:
1 Any white lockets or buttons, or white toes.
2 Incorrect pigment in nose leather, eye rims or paw pads.
3 Incorrect eye colour or trace of any colour other than blue.*
4 Lack of contrast between body colour and points.*

*Judges to exercise their discretion in respect of (3) and (4), having due regard to the normal development of eye and points colour in colourpointed kittens.

OTHERS

Pewter Exotic (70:73)
Colour: White, evenly shaded with black giving the overall effect of a pewter mantle. Legs shaded with black with undercoat, chin and stomach to be white.
Eyes: Copper, orange or deep gold.
Nose Leather: Brick red outlined with black.
Paw Pads (and visible skin on eyelids): Black or dark brown.

Additional Faults:
1 Heavy tabby markings.
2 Brown or cream tarnishing.

Blue Pewter Exotic (70:73a)
Colour: White, evenly shaded with blue giving the overall effect of a pewter mantle. Legs shaded with blue but undercoat, chin and stomach to be white.
Eyes: Copper, orange or deep gold.
Nose Leather and Paw Pads: Blue.

Additional Fault: Heavy tabby markings.

Golden Exotic (70:74)
Colour: The undercoat apricot deepening to gold. Chin, stomach and chest pale apricot; rims of eyes, lips and nose outlined with seal brown or black. Back, flanks, head and tail any shade of gold sufficiently tipped with seal brown or black to give a golden appearance; the general tipping effect to be much darker than the Tipped Exotic. Legs maybe shaded; back of legs from paw to heel solid colour or seal brown or black.
Eyes: Green or blue-green.
Nose Leather: Brick red outlined with black or seal brown.
Paw Pads: Seal brown or black.

Additional Fault: Barring on body or legs (in adults).
Note: Golden kittens often show tabby markings and may be of unsound colour.

Shaded Silver Exotic (70:75)
Colour: Undercoat pure white with black tipping shading down from the back to the flanks and lighter on the face and legs. Face and above tail must be tipped. Chin, chest, stomach, inside of the legs and underside of the tail must be pure white. The general effect to be a darker cat then the Tipped. The tipping can be one-third of the complete hair length and must be as even as possible. Hair on the footpad to the joint may be shaded to black. Legs to be the same tone as the face. Rims of the eyes, lips and nose must be outlined in black.
Eyes: Emerald green or blue-green.
Nose Leather: Brick red
Paw Pads: Black or seal brown.

Additional Faults:
1 Barring on the legs.
2 Tabby markings with the exception of ghost tail rings which should not penalise an otherwise good exhibit.

Shaded Blue Silver Exotic (70:75a)
Colour: Undercoat pure white with blue tipping shading down from the back to

Orange Eyed White male, Ch Victorious Springsteen, owned by Selina Walker.
Springsteen won Best in Show at Britain's first breed show for Exotics in 1994.

Shaded Silver Exotic female(below) and
Silver Tabby Variant male (above).

the flanks and lighter on the face and legs. Face and above side of tail must be tipped. Chin, chest, stomach, inside of the legs and underside of the tail must be pure white. The general effect to be a darker cat than the Tipped. The tipping can be one-third of the complete hair length and must be as even as possible. Hair on the footpad to the joint may be shaded to blue. Legs to be the same tone as the face. Rims of the eyes, lips and nose must be outlined in blue.

Eyes: Copper, orange or deep gold.

Nose Leather and Paw Pads: Blue.

Additional Faults:

1 Barring on the legs.

2 Tabby markings with the exception of ghost tail rings which should not penalise an otherwise good exhibit.

ailments

With a bit of luck and good care, your Exotic will live into its teens without incurring any major medical problems. However, any cat can be taken ill or receive an injury, no matter how well cared for, so it is important to know something of the most common ailments. It is also imperative to remember that your Exotic will stay in good health only if it receives annual booster vaccinations and health checks from your vet. The following is a list of the most common problems; it is by no means comprehensive and is a guide only. If you are ever worried about your cat, see a vet as soon as possible.

Abscess: A collection of pus under the cat's skin, showing as a lump which can be either hard or soft to the touch, depending on whether or not it is mature. The cause is usually an infected wound, in particular small puncture wounds which often result from fights with other cats. An abscess needs to be drained and flushed out, and probably the cat will have to be treated with antibiotics.

Allergies: Your cat can be allergic to certain substances; for example, to particular food, cigarette smoke or strong perfumes. Air fresheners and household cleaning substances can also trigger an allergy. The cat may develop skin problems and/or itchiness, sneeze or develop sore, runny eyes. If you suspect your cat has an allergy, see your vet.

Anal Glands: The cat has two small sacs located each side of its anus. When the cat sprays urine, a fluid is expelled from these sacs. On occasion, they may become impacted and cause the cat distress. This problem is much rarer in cats than in dogs, so many owners (and even vets) fail to spot the symptoms that indicate anal gland inflammation. The cat licks its lower abdomen and the inside of its hindlegs, sometimes hard enough to cause bald patches to appear. Treatment includes the manual emptying of the sacs, so see your vet.

'Black Chin': This problem is also referred to as 'greasy chin'. The cat's chin becomes greasy and the fur is matted with a heavy black substance. The skin underneath is sore and may become infected if left untreated. The cause is believed to be a yeast infection. To treat it wash the cat's chin with surgical spirit and then apply an anti-fungal cream from the vet. Treatment may need to be kept up for some weeks to be effective. Use a flea comb to remove the black grease from the hairs, to prevent re-infection.

Blocked Tearducts: Runny eyes are more or less normal in Exotics, but occasionally they may suffer from blocked tearducts. If the fluid from the eyes

page 127: Milagro Bambino, owned and bred by Christina Carpenter, shows off his magnificent eyes. Often, Exotics have a slight discharge from their eyes, but do not worry about this unless the amount of fluid suddenly increases. Photograph by Alan Robinson.

Exotics like Rojodanco Beni are lovely to cuddle but, on a practical note, the more you handle your cat, the sooner you will notice any differences in its physical appearance.

suddenly increases and seems to overflow from the eye itself (without the eye appearing sore), then a blockage may be the cause. Your vet will put the cat under general anaesthetic to clear the blockage, which is a fairly minor procedure.

Constipation: Cats become constipated for several reasons. Your cat might have swallowed something which has blocked the intestine or there may be an underlying bowel problem. Signs of constipation include a hard, swollen stomach sensitive to the touch, appetite loss, straining to go to toilet but producing very few, hard motions, no motions at all, or even a few drops of diarrhoea. A severely-constipated cat must be treated by the vet, but a couple of spoonfuls of medicinal paraffin oil may cure a milder case. If the problem recurs, the cat's diet may need adjusting, with extra fibre added to each meal.

Cystitis: Cystitis usually occurs in neutered females. The cat visits its litter tray frequently, strains when trying to urinate, and passes only a few drops. It may urinate in unusual places such as the sink. Blood may be present. Cystitis may be caused by an infection, or the cat may have abstained from urinating for a longer period than usual, causing the urine in the bladder to become stale. It is important for a vet to examine the cat, as cystitis could be confused with the similar, but much more serious, Feline Urological Syndrome (FUS).

Dandruff: Most cases of dandruff stem from incorrect diet, so a change to a suitable, good-quality diet may be all that is needed, along with a bath. If the diet is not the cause, then the dandruff may be caused by the *Cheyletiella* mite, also known as 'walking dandruff'. This mite may or may not cause itching, and it may affect just one cat, or all belonging to the same owner. It may even be confined to just one part of the cat's body, such as the ears. If *Cheyletiella* is suspected, several medical baths will be necessary, or treatment with a very powerful anti-parasitic drug, which can be either injected or given by mouth.

Diarrhoea: Pedigree cats seem to be more susceptible to diarrhoea than the ordinary moggy. Diarrhoea can be caused by stress, by a change in diet and, frequently, by drinking cow's milk. It can be a symptom of several other diseases so, if you are unsure, see the vet. For mild cases, starve the cat for 24 hours so that the stomach is given a chance to rest. Make sure that the cat has plenty of water as it may otherwise dehydrate, which is potentially fatal. (A dehydrated cat loses the elasticity of its skin, so when the skin at the scruff of the neck is pinched, it stays in place instead of quickly falling back into position.) If the diarrhoea seems to have settled after 24 hours, introduce small quantities of boiled fish or chicken, gradually increasing the portions as the cat recovers. Once back to normal, introduce a small part of the usual food into the chicken or fish.

Hilal Katy is protected against illness by annual inoculations.
Photograph by Alan Robinson.

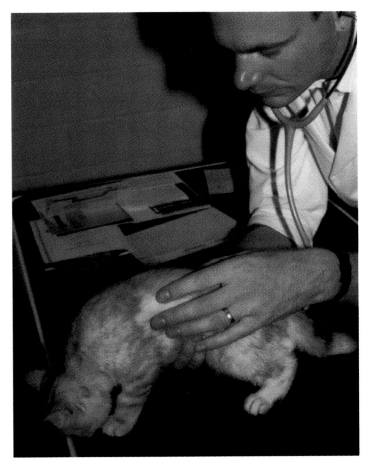

The veterinary surgeon will check your cat each time you take
it to the surgery.

Ears: Cat can suffer from earmites, yeast infections and various ear
inflammations. An over-production of wax, which is grey and very greasy, is
common in breeds with a lot of fur inside their ears, but not so much in the Exotic.
Wipe away the wax with a damp piece of cotton wool or a proprietary ear wipe
(available from pet shops and veterinary surgeries), but do not clean the ear canal
itself, as this only stimulates the production of even more wax. If the cat scratches
its ear, holds it folded down, or if any discharge can be seen, then the exact cause
needs to be found for effective treatment to be administered, so see a vet. A yeast
infection is brown in colour and causes little discomfort, but must be treated as it
may become worse.

Earmites, which usually are seen only in cats with outdoor access, cause a dark brown, nearly black, waxy discharge in the ear, which may cause the cat so much discomfort that it scratches the ear until it bleeds. If left untreated, the eardrum may become damaged. To treat both conditions, administer ear drops daily, and clean the ear carefully every second or third day.

Eyes: If the eye becomes infected for any reason, the eyelids will look red, the normal discharge will increase and probably turn to yellow or green pus. The cat keeps the eye closed. As a first step, make up a solution of one teaspoonful of boric acid powder completely dissolved into half a cup of boiling water. Allow the solution to cool to blood temperature and apply a few drops to each eye with an eye dropper. Wipe away the excess liquid with a piece of dry cotton wool. Repeat this twice a day. In many cases, the eye will show a marked improvement after only a few hours. If no improvement is noticed after 24 hours, see a vet for treatment. Boric acid can also be used for removing the brown stains underneath the eyes in pale-coated Exotics. Make a paste of boric acid powder and a little bit of previously-boiled water. Apply this to the fur underneath the eye, leave overnight and wipe away.

A dark brown speck on your cat's eye may indicate corneal necrosis, a condition believed to be hereditary, and which is sometimes seen in Persians and Exotics. If left untreated, eventually the patch covers the entire eye, rendering the cat blind. Affected cats need to be treated surgically, and should not be bred from.

Feline Calicivirus (CV) and Feline Viral Rhinotracheitis (FVR): These two viral infections are commonly referred to as cat flu, and can be prevented by annual vaccination. Even cats kept permanently indoors are susceptible to viral infections, so vaccination is essential. The diseases are highly contagious and may be fatal. The incubation period is only around a week, and symptoms include sneezing, runny eyes, discharge from the nose, swollen glands and appetite loss. If cat flu is suspected, see a vet immediately.

Feline Infectious Enteritis (FIE): FIE, also known as Feline Panleucopaenia, is entirely preventable by means of vaccination. It is highly contagious and almost always fatal. Infected cats may die without ever having shown any symptoms, and most cats die within 24 hours to one week. The virus can survive in the environment for up to three months. Symptoms include diarrhoea, vomiting, dehydration, stomach pain and severe depression.

Feline Infectious Peritonitis (FIP): FIP is a dread disease for which there is no cure and no vaccine. It is caused by a virus and seems to be more common in cats under three years of age. Symptoms may include lethargy, loss of appetite,

Our pets should be lifetime companions. A well-cared-for Exotic can live for 12–15 years. It is up to you to make sure these are happy years.

weight loss and occasionally the abdomen may appear swollen, or the breathing may become strained. The only positive diagnosis is by post mortem performed after the cat's death. A live cat can be blood tested for the presence of antibodies against the virus, which usually gives a fair idea of whether or not it is incubating the disease. Always consult your vet if you suspect FIP.

Feline Immunodeficiency Virus (FIV): Also known as Feline AIDS, FIV cannot be cured and there is as yet no vaccine available. An infected cat may not show any signs of disease in the early stages, so a blood test is the only way to find out whether or not it is infected. Therefore, it is important to test any cat that is to be mated, or any new cat coming into your household. FIV is spread primarily by biting, so outdoor cats are most at risk, especially in an area with a high proportion of strays. FIV suppresses the cat's immune system, making it susceptible to disease and unable to control any infections. Common signs of FIV include weight loss, lethargy, loss of appetite and so on, and the cat may be chronically unwell in any of a number of ways. Death is inevitable, although an infected cat may live for years before showing any signs of the disease. FIV cannot be transferred to humans or other animals.

Feline Leukaemia Virus (FeLV): Nowadays, FeLV can be prevented by an annual vaccination. However, as it is spread mainly through mating and contact with saliva, there is little or no need to vaccinate an indoor cat who has no contact with outdoor cats. Every breeding cat should be blood-tested for the presence of FeLV prior to mating. FeLV causes several different types of leukaemia, so symptoms may vary, but can include vomiting, diarrhoea, weight loss, poor appetite and breeding problems. No cure is available for infected cats.

Feline Urological Syndrome (FUS): This is fairly common and may be confused with cystitis, but FUS is much more serious and potentially fatal. It is an inflammation of the bladder and the urethra, and grain-like crystals form in the urine. These grains eventually block the urethra, preventing the cat from urinating. It is more common in males because the male's urethra is longer and of a different shape to the female's. The causes of FUS vary and are not always known. Certain types of food may have an influence, and cats prone to FUS should be put on a special diet. Signs of FUS include the cat trying to pass urine frequently, and straining but with little or no urine being passed. The cat licks its private parts, may be in obvious pain and blood may be visible. In severe cases, the cat may be lethargic, refuse to eat and have a swollen abdomen as the stale urine starts to poison it. The bladder may burst. The cat needs to be treated by the vet immediately and the bladder emptied under general anaesthetic.

Fleas: A flea infestation is probably the most common problem that your cat will encounter. Even cats kept permanently indoors may contract fleas. Signs are scratching and the tell-tale small, black specks of flea dirt left in the cat's fur, which are particularly visible in a pale-coated cat. If you rub it, the dirt turns red. You may also see live fleas on the cat's coat. There are several types of flea treatment, from collars (not recommended for show cats as they damage the neck fur), to flea sprays and tablets to put in the cat's food. Always treat the cat's surroundings with sprays as fleas and their eggs will be present in carpets and furniture. Ask your vet for advice. It is important to try to eradicate fleas. Some cats have an allergy to the bites and develop skin infections, and if the cat swallows any fleas, it may catch tapeworm.

Fur Balls: A cat is a very clean creature and constantly washes itself so, inevitably, it swallows some fur. This fur eventually forms into a ball inside its stomach. In many cases, the cat disposes of the ball by vomiting, usually after having eaten some grass. If the fur ball remains in the stomach, the cat may develop a problem, vomiting and/or losing weight. See the vet who will prescribe treatment or, in bad cases, remove the fur ball surgically.

Gingivitis: Gingivitis is an inflammation of the cat's gums, which become red, sore and bleed easily. The cat also suffers from bad breath. The commonest cause is tartar; a hard, brown matter which develops on most cats' teeth in due course. If not removed, the tartar eventually pushes up the gums, causing inflammation and tooth loss. You can prevent tartar developing by giving the cat plenty of hard food to eat, but sooner or later all cats develop it. This then has to be removed, either under anaesthetic by the vet, or (if the cat lets you) by you scraping off the tartar with a dental tooth scraper. Gingivitis needs to be treated by the vet.

Kidney Disease: Kidney disease is quite common in cats, and there are two different types: acute and chronic. Acute kidney disease is most often seen in younger cats, usually under six years old. It appears suddenly and is often fatal. The causes can vary, but can include infection or poisoning. The cat refuses to eat but still appears hungry. It may drink more or less than usual. It vomits and is lethargic and urinates more frequently. Its coat looks unkempt and it may become dehydrated. If you suspect acute kidney disease, contact your vet immediately. Urgent treatment is vital.

Chronic kidney disease mainly affects older cats, and may be more difficult to detect as the symptoms develop over a long period of time, sometimes several years. Symptoms include the cat drinking more than usual, having strong-smelling urine, urinating more frequently, vomiting occasionally, the fur losing condition, the cat losing weight. Over a prolonged period of time, the cat becomes thinner and thinner. Treatment can be very effective, and includes putting the cat on a low-protein, kidney-friendly diet which may prolong its life by several years.

Ringworm: Ringworm is not actually a worm at all, but a fungal infection. Signs include skin lesions and fur loss, with or without an accompanying itch. The lesions are seen mainly on the cat's face, back and legs. If you suspect ringworm, the vet is the only person who can make a positive diagnosis. Pregnant queens cannot be dosed with tablets so the problem is more difficult to overcome. The cat's surroundings also need to be treated, usually washed and/or sprayed with a suitable disinfectant, and all bedding washed. There is no need to shave off the cat's fur, as this irritates the cat's skin and may worsen the problem. The spores of the fungus will be present on the cat's fur, but baths twice a week for several weeks should get rid of them. A cat with ringworm should be quarantined and you should avoid contact with other cats as the spores can be carried on clothing. The spores are very resilient and may be active for as long as two years.

Treatment includes the application of a prescribed cream, and all the cats in the household must be treated with baths, creams and anti-fungal tablets. The fungus is transferable to humans (especially children) and other animals. If a human contracts ringworm, circular, red patches appear on the skin, which itches badly.

Skin Cancer: Skin cancer is common in cats with white ears that spend a lot of time in the sun. The disease begins with the cat getting sunburnt ears, the tips becoming red and sore and eventually bleeding. In time, the edges of the ears become dry, flaky and bleed frequently. The whole ear may turn cancerous and the only way of treating the cat successfully is to surgically remove part of the ear. Prevention is better than cure, so keep cats with white ears out of the sun as far as possible, or apply a high factor sunblock to the ears every day.

Stud Tail: This condition frequently occurs in stud cats, but can be seen in queens and neutered cats. The cat has a gland at the base of the tail which becomes overactive, producing a lot of greasy matter, making the tail look very unkempt. Most breeders have their own particular cure for stud tail, the most common of which seems to be washing the tail in washing-up liquid to remove the grease. However, this is not totally satisfactory and you may want to ask your vet for advice. Leave the tail alone as much as possible, as washing and brushing it only stimulates the production of the grease.

Vomiting: Cats vomit for many reasons. It can be a symptom of other diseases, or the result of a fur ball in the stomach; some cats vomit simply because their food is too cold. If your cat vomits infrequently, perhaps once a month, and appears healthy otherwise, there is no need for concern. If there is any other problem, such as the cat losing weight, developing diarrhoea or going off its food, contact a vet.

Worms: Worm infestation is common in cats, whether they are kept in or allowed outdoors. The two most common types are the roundworm and the tapeworm. The roundworm is long, thin and round, whereas the tapeworm is flat and

'Aren't I beautiful?' With help from you, your Exotic, like Garlianna Miss SoSo owned by Mrs E Dolan, will stay as beautiful as when you got it. Photo by E Dolan.

consists of several small segments. Tapeworm is usually contracted through a flea infestation. Roundworm is less commonly seen in indoor cats. Signs of worms may include a distended belly on a thin body, poor coat, appetite loss and diarrhoea. In the case of tapeworm, small grain-like worm segments can be found around the cat's tail and also in its sleeping area. Treatment is by tablets but over-the-counter remedies tend to be less effective than those obtained from the vet. These days, worming tables are available that kill off both sorts of worm in a single dose.

Wounds: Hopefully, the average indoor cat will never contract any wounds, but fights can occur at any time, especially if the cats are allowed to roam freely outside. Any wound must be washed and disinfected immediately to prevent it from becoming infected and an abscess from forming. A wound large enough to require stitches should be treated within six hours of the injury occurring but, if you are unsure whether or not it needs stitching, see your vet.

my cat's health record

Dates of first vaccinations . . . .
. . . .
Feline Influenza . . . .
. . . .
Feline Infectious Enteritis . . . .
. . . .
Annual booster due every . . . .
. . . .
Worming tablets given . . . .
. . . .
Birth of first litter . . . .
. . . .
Number of Kittens . . . .
. . . .
Date neutered . . . .
. . . .
Name, address and phone number of vet . . . .
. . . .
. . . .
Date of visit to the vet, and treatments prescribed . . . .
. . . .
. . . .
. . . .
Preferred cat sitters . . . .
. . . .
. . . .
. . . .
Preferred catteries . . . .
. . . .
. . . .
. . . .

useful addresses

As an Exotic owner interested in showing, you will find it of benefit to join a cat club or two. As the officers of the various breed and area clubs change regularly, your best option is to get in touch with the major bodies and request a list of affiliated clubs. The addresses of the major bodies in Britain and the United States can be found below.

Great Britain

The Governing Council of the Cat
    Fancy (GCCF)
4–6 Penel Orlieu
Bridgwater
Somerset TA6 3PG

The Cat Association of Britain (CA)
Show Division
10 Lyncroft Gardens
Ewell Village
Epsom KT17 1UR

United States

The Cat Fanciers' Association (CFA)
1805 Atlantic Avenue
PO Box 1005
Manasquan
New Jersey 08736-1005

American Cat Fanciers' Association
    Inc. (ACFA)
PO Box 203
Point Lookout
Missouri 65726

The American Cat Association Inc.
    (ACA)
8101 Katherine Avenue
Panorama City
California 91402

Cat Fanciers' Federation Inc. (CFF)
PO Box 661
Gratis
Ohio 45330

The Independent Cat Association
    (TICA)
PO Box 2988
Harlingen
TX 87550

index

constipation 80, 130
contractions 84, 88
corneal necrosis 133
cystitis 130

D

dandruff 130
deformities 88–89
dehydration 130
diarrhoea 130
diet sheet 26
Donceur Cheeky Charlie 15

E

ears 26, 31, 52, 62, 100, 132
  mites 32, 132–133
entry form 59–61
eyes 2, 26, 31–32, 52, 100, 133
  blocked tearducts 128
  discharge 31–32, 128, 133

F

faults (see also colours) 48, 70
Feline Calicivirus (FCV) 133
Feline Infectious Enteritis (FIE) 33, 133
Feline Immunodeficiency Virus (FIV) 32, 75, 135
Feline Infectious Peritonitis (FIP) 75, 133–134
Feline Influenza (cat flu) 33, 133
Feline Leukaemia Virus (FeLV) 32, 33, 75, 135
Feline Panleucopaenia 33, 133

Feline Urological Syndrome (FUS) 41, 42, 130, 135
Feline Viral Rhinotracheitis (FVR) 33, 133
fleas 32, 36, 62, 81, 135–136
food and nutrition 39–46
  bowls 35
  canned 43
  dried 43
  kitten 45–46, 90
  special diets 40
'frog legs'(twisted hindlegs) 89
fur 8, 20, 30, 52, 54
fur ball 41, 136

G

genetics 77
gestation 84
gingivitis 136
grooming 20, 30–38, 61–62
guard hairs 62

H

head 48–49, 100
heart murmur 89
history 10–15

I

Icemoor Barney Rubble 15
insurance 18

K

kidney disease 136

kitten development 89–90
kittening bed 83
Krissan Betty Boop 15

L

legs and paws 100
life span 18, 32
limited stud
line breeding 78
litter tray 28, 35, 90
longevity 18

M

mating 80–81
milk 43, 83, 130
minerals 42

N

nails 32, 36, 62
neutering 24, 33–34
number tally 65, 67

O

obligate carnivore 40
Owletts Maverick 15

P

pedigree
pet quality
pinking up 81
placenta 86

Pometta Strawbry Shortcake 15
points system 68, 101
powder grooming 30–31
prefix 91
pregnancy 81–83
Preliminary status 10
protein 40
Provisional status 12, 15

Q

quality 21–23, 48
queen 24, 75

R

recognition 10, 15
registration 56–57, 90–91
  Active 25, 74
  Non-active 25, 74
ringworm 26, 136–137
Robwen Cream Cracker 15
roundworm 137–138

S

scale of points 101
scratching post 36
shampoo 31
shows 15, 54–58, 65–68, 69, 70
show equipment 64–65, 67
show schedule 57–58
skin 62
skin cancer 137
slicker brush 30
Soulsease Starborn 15
Soulsease Sin Tillate 15

spraying 34
stud 34, 77–79, 91–96
stud tail 137
sunburn

T

13-day rule 61
tail 100
tail defect 48
tapeworm 137–138
teeth 136
taurine 40
temperament 8, 20, 25, 34, 40
titles 68–70,
twisted hindlegs 89
toys 36–37
type 48–49

U

ultra type 48–49
undershot bite 48, 49, 52
United States 10,

V

vaccination 25, 33, 75, 90, 128
Variants 23, 77, 90
veterinary bedding 84
vetting-in 65–67
  card
Victorious Springsteen 15
vitamins 40, 42
vomiting 137

W

water 28, 35, 43
weaning
weight 86, 88
worms 26, 137–138
wounds 138

Y

York Oliver Lawson 15